the
human
services
an introduction

the
human
services
an introduction

alice h. collins

the odyssey press
a division of
the bobbs-merrill company, inc.
indianapolis & new york

*to jean s. wilson,
great teacher and dear friend*

Library of Congress Cataloging in Publication Data
Collins, Alice H.
The human services.

Includes bibliographies.
1. Social workers.   2. Social service.
3. Social work as a profession.   I. Title.
HV41.C565   361'.0023   72–10176
ISBN 0–672–53081–3
ISBN 0–672–63081–8 (pbk)

contents

the
human
services
an introduction

author's note

Credit has been graciously given to the authors and publishers who permitted their materials to be quoted in this book. It is regrettable that thanks cannot be specifically expressed here to many others who permitted the use of their case records and to those who were willing to talk to the author about their experiences with the human services. But anonymity was the only condition they imposed in exchange for sharing their thoughts with readers. Their contributions, then, under the ambiguous title "unpublished interview," are hereby gratefully acknowledged.

introduction

Behavioral science is a relative newcomer to the scientific field. Psychology, anthropology, and sociology were not even named, much less seriously studied, until the nineteenth century, while man has systematically investigated his physical world since ancient times. Today, through observation, experiment, and painstaking checking of theory under all conditions, physical scientists can make predictions with a high degree of assurance that what is expected to happen *will* happen, regardless of time or place. Sulphur burning coal, in certain concentrations, will cause air pollution whether it burns in Tokyo or New York. But although behavioral scientists have accumulated a wealth of information about human behavior and social institutions in the short years of their formal existence, they cannot yet predict with equal assurance what will happen when members of a single family meet for breakfast, nor can they say if and how this will be like or different from another family on a different street or in another city. The inability to predict behavior is as much a result of the infinite complexity of human beings and their interaction with each other and their environments as it is of the difficulty of designing experiments which involve human beings. For example, in order to test out scientifically the assumption that certain parental behavior leads to certain kinds of deviant behavior in children, one would have to subject many children and their parents to experiences deliberately devised to hurt them over a period of years. Reputable scientists would not undertake such an experiment.

But even if they cannot yet make ironclad predictions, behavioral scientists do know a great deal about human behavior and there is much interest in their findings. The mass media devote considerable space to portraying people, their culture, and their environment in this country and all over the world. How individuals develop; how they come together in groups; how they interact with each other; how they are influenced by their culture and climate; what social structures are found all over the world and what are particular to a time and place; how these thousands of different aspects of human behavior may be accounted for in theory; how theories to explain human behavior have been built, tested and rebuilt—all these are subjects of concern to laymen and scientists as never before.

Some of the answers come from the observations of theoretical social scientists and some from practitioners who are in constant contact with the individuals under study. The field of applied social science, sometimes described as the "human services," has, like theoretical social science, expanded rapidly in recent years and is in a state of constant change. Perhaps the most practical way to describe applied social science is to list some of those who act as human service workers—people with a wide range of formal training who work with other people to help them when they are having difficulties. They include psychologists, social workers, case aides, registered nurses, licensed practical nurses, nurse's aides, special education teachers, school counselors, teacher's aides, vocational rehabilitation specialists and practitioners, correctional staffs in courts and institutions, and mental health staffs in clinics and hospitals. These are only some of the constantly growing company of human service workers, recruited to meet needs which the general public recognizes exist both from its own experience and from the communications media.

The working partnership between theoretical and applied social science is today one of the most promising developments in the scientific field. Theoretical behavioral scientists are increasingly studying social phenomena identified by applied social scientists as demanding their expert attention. And applied social scientists are increasingly using problem solving techniques developed in theoretical behavioral science to permit them to make judgments about their work which can lead to its improvement. In some instances, collaboration between both branches of behavioral science is leading to deeper theoretical understanding of scientific phenomena and more effective help for individuals in need of it.

In this book the main emphasis will be on applied social science—the human services—with some discussion of the basic skills needed in both theoretical and applied social science. The book is addressed to people who are interested in learning more about working directly with people in an effort to help them solve their problems. There are, of course, many ways of doing this. The goal of changing the social conditions which give rise to personal problems might be achieved through a career in politics. Research interviewing of victims of a disabling disease might lead to its cure. This book is chiefly concerned, however, with human service workers whose job it is to help individuals through a crisis when someone who is ordinarily independent needs a lift, to offer long term help for those with severe emotional or physical handicaps, or to perform specialized services for the victims of rapid technological and social change. The great majority of human service workers are based in agencies such as mental health facilities, foster care and adoption agencies, hospitals, prisons, courts, training schools, day care centers, and public welfare agencies.

Human service workers may be givers and users of the human services at the same time. A nurse's aide may be caring for surgical patients during her working day and receiving some counseling in her time off to help her resolve a problem in her marriage, or make some decisions about care for her mentally retarded son or her elderly father. A social worker with a master's degree who supervises the work of thirty caseworkers who deal with the multiple problems of families struggling with life and death issues of food and shelter, may make grateful use of an educational aide in the nursery school attended by her four-year-old daughter.

When formal human services first began to grow out of the neighborliness and mutual help systems of a largely rural population, they were organized and supported by well-to-do people, often religiously motivated, who saw the needs of the poor and the danger of permitting those needs to go unmet. As the behavioral sciences developed, so did public understanding and concern for individuals with problems of dependency, illness, and deviance. Social conditions frequently separated individuals from their usual caregivers, their families, and presented them with the difficulties of dealing with life in large cities sometimes far from their own countries and customs. Many new problems of housing, employment, health, and interpersonal relations had to be resolved. The demands on agencies for help in these matters rapidly outgrew the resources of private support. Public funds had to be allocated and many more human service workers had to be recruited. Agencies reflected the changes in American society too, not only in the way they were financed but also in the services they offered. Where once, for example, there were many agencies devoted to assisting in the assimilation of immigrants from Europe to the large cities in this country, today these have practically disappeared, and new agencies are attempting to provide long overdue help to some groups of native Americans. Where once children whose parents could not or would not care for them were placed in orphanages, today such children are cared for in adoptive or foster homes. Where once only a very few agencies were needed to care for the elderly because life spans were short and only the destitute without family ties were in need of agency intervention, today improved health care and changes in life style and social customs have brought about many agencies organized especially to meet the needs of elderly people of all social classes.

When social agencies were first organized most of their work was

done by unpaid volunteers or low-salaried people whose chief qualification was an enthusiastic interest. No one expected them to accomplish miracles. But, as agencies grew and changed, they required
an increasing number of human service workers. The human services began to attract people with advanced education and training
and to expect a constantly higher level of both. As more public
money was invested in the human services, public expectations
grew as to what human service workers were expected to accomplish. Higher training standards were set up in an effort to make the
human services more effective and efficient.

More recently, the new trend in human service agencies repre-
sents a combination of two different attitudes toward the background requirements for human service workers. It is held that an
agency is more effective if it includes human service workers from
a wide range of experience, training, age, sex, and color. School
principals have found that some students who do not learn from a
teacher with a graduate degree may respond to a neighborhood
housewife with a high school education; nurses and doctors know
that patients who seem unable to cooperate in their care, even with
the most sophisticated medical procedures, may improve if a
nurse's aide gives them a great amount of individualized attention.
Recreational agencies have sometimes discovered the reverse—that
a doctoral candidate in psychology who cannot throw a ball straight
can give advice about a playground program that will increase its
usefulness manyfold. What seems to work best is a partnership of
helping people with varying degrees of training and experience,
sharing an interest in one another's chosen tasks and skills. Most
forward-looking human service agencies now include this variety
among the helping people on their staffs. It is now feasible for individuals who are interested in the possibilities of a career in human
service to test out their interest in a number of ways and at a number of levels.

An individual believing himself to have an interest or aptitude
in working with children may, in addition to formal study, become
a part-time or full-time case aide in a school for mentally retarded
children. He may find that he has a special talent for working with
these children and a particular interest in this important and as yet
undeveloped field. He may want to go on to learn more about the
mentally retarded in a formal educational program, or he may decide to learn of other fields of care to determine whether he likes
those as well. He may decide to go on to full professional training
in education, social work, pediatric nursing, or psychological research, perhaps specializing in the mentally retarded or in some

other aspect of child welfare. Or he may decide that having discovered a field of service he likes, he does not want to leave it to
get additional formal education. He will still have the daily opportunity to learn more by experience, to test out what he has learned,
to increase his skills, and to help teach them to others. Whatever
direction he chooses to take he may have the satisfaction of knowing that he is helping others while doing what he wants to do and
does well.

Today there are many people, young and older, who are interested in the human services at every career level. They want to
know more about them—what kinds of skills are required, what
kind of people and conditions are to be met there, what human
service workers think about the work, favorable and unfavorable.
This book is intended to answer some of their questions. Part One
discusses some general aptitudes and skills which are basic to success in all the human services and then goes on to present a variety
of aspects of the work itself. People of different ages, ethnic origins
and with a varying degree of problems are to be met in Part Two
where both givers and users of services are introduced, often in the
first person, but sometimes as seen through the eyes of others. An
attempt has been made to discuss the settings in which the problems
are met because, as has been said above, most human formal services are carried on in agencies.

No manageable book could hope to show all the human settings
and all kinds of human service workers any more than it could discuss in any detail the many different techniques that are based on
the skills briefly described in Part One. Some way of dividing the
material had to be found for the convenience of the reader. The
chapters in Part Two, therefore, are focused around the broad categories of those making use of the services—children, families,
groups in the communities that surround them, and individuals in
institutions who are temporarily or permanently separated from
their families. Of course, the reader should keep in mind that these
are artificial separations. In reality, one person might be placed in
one or all of these categories or, as has been pointed out, be both a
human service worker and a user of human services.

Readers who find themselves in agreement with some of the people herein, who discovered that they did not like the human services
or had little aptitude for work in them, will also profit by discover-
ing this fact early in their search for a career. While, for those who
enjoy them, the human services offer a great deal of satisfaction,
there is in fact no greater virtue in being a nurse, a nurse's aide, or
a mental health worker than there is in being an engineer who de-

signs an efficient hospital for them to work in or a medical techni-
cian who tests procedures vital to patients' recovery but who never
has personal contact with patients.

Hopefully the following pages will help the reader to a greater
understanding of the human services.

| part one | *human service tasks and skills* |

1 | *the signal system*

This chapter will discuss in general terms the tasks human service workers are expected to perform and the basic skills needed to carry them out. It will give the reader an opportunity to judge for himself if he has the interest and talent necessary to develop these skills which are demonstrated in Part Two.

What society expects of the human service worker, what he expects of himself, and what those he serves expect of him are all the same—that he bring about behavioral change. But it is not necessarily true that they all agree on what kind of change is desirable. Society may demand that the human service worker reform the delinquent boy so that his behavior will no longer be troublesome to law abiding people. The human service worker may want to see changes in the school system or the state laws to prevent an individual from becoming delinquent. At the same time he may want the individual to change so that he may enjoy the same freedom as most boys and girls. The delinquent himself may want the human service worker to change the behavior of others toward himself. All human service workers have the same rights and responsibilities as other citizens in helping to bring about change which will help all people to live happier and more productive lives. These goals are the specific ones of some human service workers also. But on the whole, the daily work of most human service workers, especially those first entering the field, is concerned with helping other people change their behavior, rather than with helping social institutions to change their point of view or the social system.

Before the human service worker can begin to learn how to help people change behavior, he needs to be sure he knows what behavior is. In general, behavior may be said to be the action of living things in response to the impact of the environment upon their innate, inherited characteristics.

In a seed packet environment, plant seeds are specks of inert matter. Their behavior changes dramatically when they are placed on a bit of wet cotton. When they are planted in the ground where they have light and water, they behave entirely differently than they did in the seed packet or on the cotton. Too much water may kill them; too much or too little light may make for distortion of

11

growth; soil compatible with the characteristics transmitted to them from endless generations of ancestors will cause them to behave in one way; soil not suited to their inbred needs or to the conditions of light and water that exist may cause them to behave differently. So even plants, which are generally agreed to be "simple" forms of life as compared with human beings, modify their behavior in response to the interplay of many forces. This makes it hard to know at a glance what their behavior signifies and what can be done to change it. Hundreds of garden columns and garden books are based on this difficulty!

The relative immobility of plants contrasts with the mobility of animals who may, therefore, be expected to be influenced by more kinds of outer conditions and to respond with a much greater range of behavior to these influences. The more highly developed the animal, the more capacity he has for reasoning, and for responding to stimuli which now are not only the physical environment but the emotional environment as well. Only a very few people believe that plants will respond to kind or angry words from their caretaker. But no one who has known a dog will question that his feelings influence his behavior. The presence or absence of his master, for example, may affect his appetite. He behaves with every evidence of pleasure in contact with some individuals and with hostility or avoidance with others. Perceptive dog owners can usually, but not always, predict how their dogs will behave under certain conditions but outsiders who have not known the animal from puppyhood, or who have paid little attention to dogs in the past, will find much of the behavior they may note impossible to explain. Why does he run back and forth whining when his owner goes to the door; why does he persistently nudge the stranger who sits in a certain armchair; why does he crawl abjectly under the bed when a suitcase is brought out of a closet?

If it is difficult to understand animal behavior, it is infinitely more so to understand human behavior. It is known that human beings receive at least twenty-three chromosomes from each parent and that each chromosome carries at least one gene, the cells of which are known to be the carriers of human inherited characteristics. Mathematically, the number of combinations possible from this simple set of figures approaches infinity, which means that no two individuals have exactly the same inherited characteristics.

And from the moment of conception, no two individuals are exposed to exactly the same physical environment, nor are they, as they grow from babyhood, exposed to exactly the same social conditions. Even identical twins, whose physical heritage is the only exception to the rule of inherited differences, are inevitably treated a little differently from infancy, a difference which is likely to grow wider as they mature. A first-born child does not have the same family as the youngest child, nor of those in between. Human beings grow up through constantly changing environmental experiences which impinge on their developing inherited characteristics. Their behavior in the present is the response to an immediate stimulus, colored by their unique experiences in the past. Theories of human personality development and interpretations of human behavior vary in the weight that is attached to hereditary influences, to the impact of the environment, and to the present stimuli. They vary in the way in which they consider behavior may be influenced. But almost all widely credited theories today acknowledge that human behavior is a response to the interaction of heredity and environment.

To state it even more simply: human behavior has meaning, but it is not at all simple to know what specific behavior means. And this is no less true of one's own behavior than that of others. Behavior can be thought of as a signal system. Sometimes the signals are understood by all those who receive them, sometimes only by those who have the code. The cry of an infant may tell anyone who hears him that he wants something, but his mother can tell at once whether he is hungry, wet, or wants company. And probably every normal adult has had the experience of behaving in ways he cannot logically explain. "How could I have forgotten that important appointment?", "what in the world made me do such a thing?", or "why do I always act this way with her?" are familiar self-questions that are rarely answered easily. One might say the behavior here is a signal in a code to which the sender has no key. He has both received and sent out a message in code. The receiver of this message may not be able to understand it either. He may attempt to read it as though it were not coded, and so get the wrong message, or he may pay little attention to it because he does not have the code to decipher it.

Appeals for help are more often than not sent in a code unintelligible to the sender. The human service worker needs to have the skill to interpret their general meaning and to act on his general understanding while he attempts to arrive at a more exact translation through a continuing relationship. A rescue operation, mounted on the basis of general understanding, may even make more painstaking decoding unnecessary by altering the conditions which stimulated the cry for help.

This is a complicated explanation for a process that is actually well known to almost everyone who has human contacts; but it is so basic to success in the human services that it deserves serious consideration.

Signals can be sent and received in many different kinds of codes —language, actions, facial and bodily expressions—separately or all at once. Even the absence of signals is a signal! Like the unheard sounds that are continually about us in the air (and perhaps in the sea), some signals can be heard and interpreted only by experts who are using highly specialized instruments. But many human behavior signals become intelligible to human service workers when they recognize them and try to understand them.

One other generalization may be made about the people to be met in the human services. The behavior that acts as a signal code is often unpleasant. People who come to the attention of human service workers do so because they are troubled, because they or people close to them feel they are unable to deal with the situations in which they find themselves, or because others insist that they must change their way of life. They are temporarily or permanently dependent on someone else to help them conduct their lives. The feelings of fear and anxiety that this often arouses are known to everyone who has experienced dependency actually or vicariously. To be at the mercy of others is to expose oneself to the possibility of defenselessness against injury.

Individuals respond differently to this sense of impending doom, but none of them put their best foot forward, are their best selves, under these circumstances. Many, even while they ask for help, loudly deny their need for it, threatening those they ask and boasting of their own strength and power; others make exaggerated gestures of conciliation and compliance indicating their non-aggression and their grateful appreciation and willingness to do what is asked of them; still others make no response at all, ignore the situation, and cover up their feelings so completely that their existence can only be seen negatively—an absence of smoke where there is known to be fire. Whatever their response to the pressures of asking for help, the people that are met by human service workers are not likely to be as easy to understand, as pleasant, and as open as they might be under different circumstances.

Of course, it is not only the receiver of the human service who is sending out behavior signals. The human service worker himself, being human, is also doing so. He, too, has a personality developed through interaction between the environment and his inherited characteristics, influenced by the culture he has grown up in as well as the one in which he meets the person in need of help. He, too, is responding to the behavior of the person he is trying to help and is sending out signals of response.

What differentiates the skilled human service worker from most other people is that he accepts the responsibility of trying to decode messages before he sends them. No one can do this completely, and to do it at all takes a great deal of effort, education, and self-discipline. But every human service worker can learn to do it to some degree and is under a moral obligation to do so. Yet, human service workers need also to be able to accept the fact that, even if they make every effort to understand their own behavior and act accordingly, they may still be misunderstood because their messages come across in garbled code.

In summary some generalizations can be made about human service workers in regard to what they will need to know about behavior. They need to recognize that they send messages constantly and that their messages may not be decoded by the receivers as saying what was intended. They need to be able to accept the possibility that their good intentions will be misunderstood or resisted and that, no matter what they do, those they seek to help may be angry, frightened, unreasonable, and undependable.

How can the individual who wants to be a human service worker prepare himself for this extremely difficult task? He can learn from theoretical formulations about human nature and human institutions in general, learning which is the speciality of the social sciences but which can be broadened by an acquaintanceship with the humanities, too. Philosophers, novelists, and artists all have insights into man and his world which can teach the human service worker much that he will find useful in practice.

Most of all, he will need to expand his native ability to do what all social scientists do—to observe and describe what he has observed so that each experience prepares him for the next. Observation and description are the tools of all human service workers—those with little formal education and those with a great deal. Skill in the use of these tools comes from education and practice. Learning, doing, reviewing action, revising what is learned, acting on the revision, and examining success or failure are as necessary to the applied social scientist as to the theoretician at every level. The repetition of these steps keeps the human service worker in touch with changes in the climate in which he works, with new learning, and with new methods and ways of adapting earlier experience, all of which make this difficult field one of life-long interest to many people.

One other factor that leads to success in the human services so defies analysis and description that it is tempting to avoid mentioning it. Its existence is familiar to anyone who has had contact with human service workers and many who know, without experience, that this will be their field of work. It can only be described by that vague term "talent." Some people have great talent for people. It seems likely that, as with any art, the people who have the talent possess a special receiving and sending system which picks up signals unseen and unheard by others. It may be that certain people become more sensitized to signal systems because of their interest in people and their inner drives toward involvement with them. These talented people are usually more anxious to learn the tools of the human services than those with less talent, because they are aware of both the need for skills and the danger of clumsiness or ignorance. The following chapters will discuss these tools.

2 | *observation*

No matter how young he is, the human service worker brings to his task a considerable experience in receiving signals through his senses. Now, he has accepted the obligation of acting on what the signals tell him. His first step must therefore be to make sure that he is receiving *all* the signals that are sent, not just those that are easily perceived by any eye or ear. Only when he is sure he has seen and heard them all as clearly and accurately as possible will he be ready to decode them, to match what his senses have told him against what he has learned from experience, specialized training, or both. Once that task of description is done, he can then move toward action based not on the snap judgment of the layman but on the consciously arrived at findings of the scientist.

Sometimes, of course, he can and must take all three steps in the space of a minute—his senses may tell him that children locked in a car while their parents work need immediate care and he will provide it almost without thinking. But the children may be in equal jeopardy tomorrow unless, once the emergency is over, he takes systematic steps to be sure that he has perceived the situation correctly and has made a judgment in accordance with all he has learned. On this basis he can make a firm plan for the solution of the problem that lies behind the need for instant action.

This chapter and the next will attempt to suggest some ways by which the human service worker can be sure he has received as many signals as possible, that he has used his senses to their fullest capability, and that he has minimized his personal blocking action.

One reason why it is hard to become a good observer is that observation is so easy and natural to everyone it is hard to take it seriously as a subject for study and training. In reality, observation is both natural and learned from infancy. The baby begins his life experience by taking things in with his eyes as well as his mouth, and by feeling, tasting, and smelling what he sees. The first lessons for baby animals are in sharpening their powers of observation which can mean the difference between life and death to them. The human mother, like the animal mother, trains her babies to observe, although perhaps neither mother is entirely aware of what she is doing. Mothers smile at their babies to awaken the answering smile. "See the toy," "pat the dog," "taste the fruit," and "smell the flower" are said in one form or other to millions of babies daily. "Discover your senses and what they can tell you" would be a rather pompous translation of this natural introduction to observational experience. It has been noted, however, that when this kind of parental direction is absent, children appear to grow with so little awareness of the world around them that they may never learn or develop normally. Whether this failure results from lack of stimulation or the absence of a loving arm around the learner is a matter for interested study at this time. But there is no doubt that an ever-increasing keenness of observation is necessary to formal learning from kindergarten through the Ph.D. and that it is the foundation on which interpersonal relations are built at all ages.

Accurate perception is also the basic qualification for many kinds of vocational activities, from aeronautics to tea tasting. Many jobs depend on accuracy of vision. Much leisure time activity too involves the ability to observe. Mystery dramas pit the viewer's or reader's powers of observation of small, cleverly hidden signals or clues against those of the hero or villain. Actors add challenge by showing through word, gesture, and appearance who they are not. And, having given a convincing performance, they often make a "personal appearance" which permits the viewer to mark the degree of their skill in sending signals which will spell out a consistent image other than the real one.

Bird watchers, rock collectors, and other naturalists make continual use of their ability to see small differences—the movement of a wing, the shadings in a stone, the smell and texture of the soil are noted by these trained observers, when to others there is nothing unusual to be seen. The human service worker will also make use of his senses, chiefly those of sight and hearing. This chapter will deal with the sense of sight and the next chapter with the function of hearing.

The first thing that anyone notes about another person is what he looks like. Billions of dollars are spent on this assumption and on the further assumption that everyone wants to put his best foot forward on first acquaintance and that if his appearance is "right" he will be comfortable himself and acceptable to others. This emphasis may well lead to exploitation, the creation of artificial standards, and the marketing of goods to meet them. But the concern people have about their appearance and its conformity with their fellows is probably based on the biological finding that social animals signal their right to peer group membership by their appearance.

When the human service worker meets an individual for the first time, he not only will want to notice his appearance but he will want to note how it fits into the usual appearance of other people of approximately the same age, sex, and place. Customs change rapidly and there are many subgroups who signal their difference from the majority and conformity with each other in the manner of their dress, grooming, and general style. The human service worker needs to keep informed about these changes as much as he can. It was no doubt easier in past generations than it is today to make distinctions between sex, age, and occupational and socioeconomic level just by observation, but there are still many differences to be noted if the human service worker is a good observer.

A sharp observer will notice many variations in the appearance of individuals who generally seem to be well matched with their fellows and "in" groups. He will easily note some incongruities in appearance—a carefully groomed middle-aged woman barefoot on a city street would be much more noticeable than a barefoot teenager in blue jeans. A man would be quickly noticed if he wore the same clothes into the swimming pool that he was wearing on the street ten minutes earlier. Extremes of behavior are, of course, easier to see. A man screaming and waving his arms in the middle of an empty street will not be overlooked. One who stands silent and unsmiling in a crowd celebrating a football victory may not be noticed. Both may be signaling that they have problems that demand attention.

Observation is so natural a thing that most people hardly know that they are observers, nor do they make an effort to assure themselves that they are really seeing what is there. Since so much depends on their observations, human service workers will do well to develop the habit of noting the different aspects of what is to be seen and mentally ticking off their findings in various categories.

What a person does, as well as what he looks like, is part of his appearance and is worth noting. In fact, *how* he does it merits attention. Hands and eyes can signal almost innumerable messages. It is now believed that from early infancy babies actually "see" the eyes of their mother before they see anything else and that early recognition of people is through recognition of their eyes. Sparkling eyes, downcast eyes, sad eyes, tender eyes appear over and over again in fiction and on the stage and screen to convey the mood of the whole person or even the plot of a story. Hands and their gestures are another such signal system universally used and universally interpreted. Hand gestures convey friendliness and hostility, submission and defiance, happiness and sadness, dependence and independence—the list is endless. Some gestures have different meanings in different cultures, but most people who watch carefully can quickly learn what a gesture means and can respond with an appropriate one.

There are body gestures, too, that the human service worker needs to train himself to note. And more particularly, he needs to note, as he does in appearance, the way the gesture fits in with other behavior or appearance. The surprise of the incongruity of action with appearance is the basis for much humor. The "sight gag" depends on the viewer's acceptance of the actor as the little, meek, weak character he appears to be. His attack on the burly hero or his advances to the gorgeous heroine are funny because they are out of character and unexpected. The human service worker is not looking to be amused but to learn what he can about the person he is trying to help. He wants, therefore, to be able to have a base for some predictions, and he needs to note all the signals which he can eventually decode into a message which will tell him what to expect.

Everyone knows that the same person looks different in different lights. Having to come to a strange place to ask for or use help is hard for everyone but especially so for people who do not have much hope of finding it. Being in a place that has its own rules and regulations with which one is unfamiliar can be upsetting in itself as anyone who has traveled in a country in which he did not speak the language can testify. One feels an "outsider" and is inclined to question the intentions of the "insiders" even if the place is a hospital whose purpose it is to help patients. People who have struggled to solve their own problems and are admitting defeat to themselves when they ask for help may even act as though their difficulties were created by the human service worker. Behavior observed under stressful conditions, then, may well seem inappropriate.

However, if the human service worker is able to adjust his sights to view the real situation, a crisis may offer him an unusually good opportunity to help. It has been noted that in a time of crisis people are shaken out of their customary ways of behaving, are bewildered and confused for a time, and then settle back into old ruts or move forward into new and better ways of functioning. It has been found that if the right kind of help is available to individuals at such a time, they are more likely to find new and more satisfying ways of life than if they have to face it alone or only with the help of others as frightened as themselves.

The human service worker also needs to recognize that sometimes the reverse may be true. In spite of his sincere desire to offer help, a person may turn away from him at first sight or in a crisis for no apparent reason. The human service worker often does not know the reasons behind this behavior, but he must remember that it is not only the setting and the personal situation of the person needing help that enters into every encounter in the human services, but that he, himself, is part of the experience. How he behaves, how he feels, what he looks like is noted, consciously or unconsciously, by the person he is seeing. Observation is a two-way occupation. The human service worker needs to practice looking at himself objectively through the eyes of the other person. He needs to consider the setting and how he looks in relation to it and to become aware of what prevailing opinions are about his job in that setting.

It is hard to remember that a setting which has become so familiar as to be almost invisible can have an effect on another person, but a continuing effort to do so is the mark of the truly observant and skilled human service worker.

senior high school:
student report

It is unlikely that his teachers and counselors saw themselves as Mike described them in the following composition. The positive response of his teacher is an indication of her skill and her willingness to learn.

Mike entered my sophomore high school class in the middle of the term and had been in it two weeks without doing anything at all when I told him, "This is it Mike. I must have some work done and turned in. You must complete your theme on *I Have a Dream* before you leave school today."

mike's theme

I have a dream of not ever having to go to school. The reasons for this are that the teachers bug me all the time and they make me do dumb stuff like writing these reports on dreams. If I work in the day time I could take a pill before going to bed and then I could be intelligent in the morning. Don't get me wrong! I am not stupid. I love to read and I can probably read faster and comprehend more than 80% or 95% of the students in my class. My problem is that I don't like sitting in cold drafty class rooms with a bunch of dumb teachers telling me what to do and where to go! One of these times I am going to tell them what to do

From an unpublished letter to the author. Used with permission.

and where to go! The counselors always tell me I am lazy and stupid when its really them who are. They take about 25 coffee breaks a day and you can never find them when you need them. When I first came to this school we went to the office. A student told us, my brother and I, to go to counselling. When we got there Mrs. Munson told us to sit down and wait for a Mr. Smith. We sat for 30 minutes. When at last Smith came and asked us what we wanted. We said we wanted to enroll. He said we needed to bring a parent.

The next try 2 days later we brought our mother. We again sat outside counselling waiting for some loudmouth counsellor. We sat for two hours and 45 minutes. At 11:30 he came and looked at us for about 2 minutes and then told Munson to show us the forms. That counsellor really must have thought he was cool because he was important enough to be waited on! Personally I don't think he was important enough to lead a herd of jackasses. These are only a few reasons why I think schools should be abolished. The End.

Observation is not something the human service worker does once and for all. He needs to develop the capacity to observe constantly and freshly, to note small changes, and to make readjustments in his behavior. This may mean that he must face the fact that the first observations he made were incomplete or erroneous. And it takes courage to be able to face one's mistakes.

Observation, which at first glance seems to be so natural and simple a matter as to need no discussion, is in fact an extremely complicated and difficult, if exciting, skill. In the hands of an inexperienced craftsman it is a crude tool; practice and training can lead to a high degree of precision.

human behavior course: melanie

The following observations about a mentally retarded teenager were written by a college freshman in a course on human behavior. Two months elapsed between the first and second reports. In both instances the girls were at a church service, and there had been few actual changes in those weeks, except that the vision of the observer had sharpened, leading to a new kind of understanding.

Melanie is mentally retarded. She is in her late teens. She is a big girl, not fat but large boned. Her appearance is always quite neat. Her short brown hair is always combed neatly. I know her

From an unpublished report. Used with permission.

from Sunday school where her mother was my teacher. Melanie comes from a strong Christian family, and has a happy home life.

two months later

In the evening service I looked at Melly, just to see what she was doing. She was sitting there next to her dad playing with her hands. She was doing the motions I learned many, many years ago—the "here's the church, here's the steeple, open the doors and see all the people."

She kept doing it over and over again through the message. I don't know what ignited her to do this—but I guess she was bored and she associated her being in church with something she had remembered.

Another thing—she didn't have an expression on her face at all. No smile, no grin, just nothing. When I was a little kid and used to do the same thing, I used to get a big kick out of it and think I was real smart. Melly just sat there—staring at her awkward hands.

It may be somewhat disconcerting to realize that there is so much more to seeing another person than one usually realizes. It may seem too much to expect that one can note so many things—general appearance; compatibility with the individual's age, sex, culture, and sub-culture; incongruities and compliances with the standards of the group; and what those standards seem to be in relation to the setting from which he comes and the one where the human service worker finds him. His actions as well as his outward appearance must be closely observed—the kind and number of gestures he uses examined just as his appearance is. And, the most difficult of all is to "see" oneself as the person may see one.

Indeed, much remains to be learned about observation but it can be said that there are great rewards for the attentive observer—in the human services and outside of them. He will find that he is more skilled at his job as he sees more, even though he may not yet try to interpret what he sees according to any systematic theory. And he may find that his ability to see more will make it easier to enjoy his contacts with some of the troublesome people he meets in his work or in his personal life.

3 | *interviewing*

Even while he is making visual observations, the human service worker will want to use another of his senses—hearing—to gain an understanding of a problem. Most often he will also make use of speech. Hearing and speaking are often thought of as one process in the human services and are referred to as interviewing. That term will be used here, too, for convenience. Since both the human service worker and the person he seeks to help can listen and/or speak, the possibilities of interaction at this level are multiplied over those already described as "seeing." Though this adds to the complexity of the human service worker's task, it also gives him greater opportunity to choose the right tool for a particular task.

Fortunately, by the time the human service worker enters the field, he has already had an extensive experience with these tools of hearing and speech and has acquired considerable skill in their use. Even before they are able to speak clearly, children discover that questions are answered and demands met differently when they are addressed to different people, and that certain conditions of time and place affect the answers likely to be forthcoming. As they grow up, they continue to make ever finer distinctions in hearing and develop the ability to distinguish between "real" questions and answers and what might be called un-questions and answers. Every child knows that "What do you want?" requires a different answer from "How are you?" and "How are you?" is a different question when asked by an adult met on the street or one met in the hospital. He knows that "Can I stay home from school?" will be answered differently from "Can I be an astronaut when I grow up?"

For very young children, speech is itself an exciting and exhilarating experience. Sounds and words are experimented with for their own sakes, regardless of meaning. But as mastery of language increases so does discrimination in its use. Quite young children learn how to answer questions selectively. "Who broke this?" can be answered directly with a confession of guilt or an accusation against someone else, or equivocally—"I don't know," or with another question—"Why ask me?", or with a lie—"I didn't do it." So, even before he goes to school the child is likely to have acquired considerable skill in asking and answering questions.

24

At school, he will refine these skills and add to them as both teacher and learner are involved in asking and answering questions, and the pupil who performs in the manner expected of him is rewarded. Here, the child is given the opportunity to learn how to ask for what he wants to know, and how to use the answers he receives. He may learn, too, how to ask and answer questions without learning and to be selective in choosing questions and answers suited to the time and place and to his social purposes, in order to evaluate his own success or failure and modify his subsequent behavior.

If the human service worker has had some work experience before entering the human services he may have an additional experience and even some formal training in asking and answering questions and hearing and responding to spoken and unspoken requests. Sales people depend on their ability as interviewers to make a living whether they sell cosmetics, gasoline, airline services, or automobiles. Research and experimentation are going on constantly to increase understanding of a process which may lead to more sales.

Those who buy as well as those who sell goods and services are today being helped to improve their interviewing skills. Consumer education programs increasingly alert consumers to ask about products and to become aware of the setting in which an interview takes place and the influence of business and social pressures.

It is paradoxical that his experience and skill may at first be a stumbling block for the human service worker. Familiarity with the process of interviewing may have led him to develop habits of listening and speaking which he continues to use without considering that they may not be suitable for the position he now holds. The best safeguard against such a blind approach is to listen to oneself hard and often, a difficult thing to do but a most useful one. It might be said in passing that one of the most valuable aids to this kind of self-analysis is a tape recorder. The human service worker who records his own interviews occasionally and then listens to the playback will quickly—and perhaps with astonishment and embarrassment—recognize some of the ways in which he can improve his use of the interviewing tools.

A frequent restatement of the goals of interviewing may also be useful for the human service worker. The acquisition of technical skill is a sterile process unless one has a goal toward which these skills are bent. Goals differ, of course, according to innumerable variables. But it is well to remind oneself that in the human services the long-range goal is to help people to live as personally satisfying and socially productive lives as they are capable of doing.

Formal, routine interviewing for the purpose of getting facts on which to base future decisions is often a first task assigned to a human service worker. He may feel that "there is nothing to it," a conclusion that seems obvious when the interviewing is intended merely to fill out a form made up of questions about facts—name, address, occupation, number of relatives, previous work experience. It is natural for the worker who may have asked these questions several hundred times to feel impatient with hesitancy in the person who must answer them before a judgment can be made as to his eligibility for help or before a referral for health, employment, or vocational rehabilitation services can be made. Yet every one of these questions may sound ominous and threatening to the hearer.

Even before the interviewer asks the first question, the kinds of answers that will be forthcoming are being conditioned. The person who is being interviewed is more than likely to be struggling with a difficult problem he cannot solve alone. It may be a new problem, related to a crisis in his life, or it may be one of long standing which has finally forced him to seek and accept help. He is likely to be painfully aware of every small detail of the place and the people he meets, as people often are when they meet new and emotion-laden situations. He may see it as unfriendly or as actively threatening and ungiving. If he has another kind of temperament, he may refuse to see the real setting at all and shut it out, either by looking at it almost blindly or distorting what he sees and hears so that it takes on a friendlier and less threatening aspect. The interviewer, on the other hand, may have helped several hundred people to fill out the forms before him; he may of necessity have only a few minutes available to him to get the answers accurately, so that he hardly looks up from the form, and if he does, he may tend to see the person he is interviewing only as a blurred composite of all the many others he has seen before. And, too, he may have some personal concerns which the questions and answers arouse. He himself may have sat on the other side of the desk only a short time ago, or a relative, loved or not loved, in a similar situation may have acted in ways that are painful to remember. It is plain, without further elaboration, that the two people involved in the simplest kind of human service interview are in a relationship which is far from simple.

Yet there is no doubt that facts must be collected if service is to be given in almost any human service setting and that the human service worker, whether beginning or experienced, will often have to ask direct questions and try to get reliable answers to them. What is he to do even if he knows that the setting leaves much to be desired and that his questions which must be answered may be heard in many ways? Curiously enough, he does not need to *do* anything different—in fact, he often has no choice in this matter and must continue to do what his job requires. What can make a difference for him and the interviewee is the development of his ear. Just as a musician learns to distinguish tones and half tones, changes of key, and shadings to which the ordinary listener is deaf, the interviewer can learn to listen for shades of difference in the first answer he gets to his first question and, without changing the words of the following questions, ask them so that they will be better heard and answered. As has been noted, this is an ability that has been developing in most normal people since early childhood.

Almost everyone can recall occasions when a friendly smile and effusive greeting meant nothing and even aroused anger or when a glance, without words, made it easier to answer a difficult question. There are many instances, too, when the human service worker does not need to follow a form but is free to carry on an unstructured interview to gather the information needed. Here the worker will learn from his own experience and that of others what words and actions on his part will yield the greatest return in adding to his understanding of need.

The more experienced the human service worker becomes, the more he is able to send and receive meaningful wordless messages. Talented human service workers naturally tune their interviewing to the needs of the person asking for help.

health center: public health nurse

The brief exchange described below was probably almost unnoticed by the public health nurse who carried it out with so sure a sense of timing. But it was certainly important to the patient and, one may surmise, was pleasantly remembered for a long time to come. The setting was a district health center on a very cold day in the midst of an epidemic of Asian flu that was especially dangerous to old people. Thousands of the elderly were in the center being immunized as rapidly as the public health nurses could work.

Most of the people had tear-filled eyes from having come through the bitter cold, and they were lining up in front of a table that held rows of plastic syringes filled with vaccine.

From *The New Yorker*, January 11, 1969, p. 25.

"You know, I'm afraid," an elderly Negro woman said as she rolled up her left sleeve.

"We're all afraid, dear," replied one of the public health nurses, swabbing the old woman's arm with alcohol and inoculating her. "There. Now it's all over and you were very brave."

This short episode illustrates still another important aspect of interviewing the human service worker may wish to consider. It is notable that the frantically busy nurse did not ignore the comment or assure the old lady that it wouldn't hurt much, remind her of all the good results that would be achieved, or tease and cajole her. In a few words she recognized her as a member of the not very courageous human race—and acted. And then, in the moment before she turned to the next old person, the nurse gave the lady friendly praise and reassurance to carry away with her. The whole episode probably consumed less than a minute and would most likely have escaped the notice of all but a very well-trained ear. Yet possibly it saved much time, as well as human dignity. Without the nurse's words, the old lady might have been overcome with her fears, have refused the injection, required time and effort at persuasion, and have set off a chain reaction in the waiting room full of apprehensive people. Instead, she took home with her a friendly, comforted feeling that would make it easier for her to seek medical help in the future.

This aspect of the human services is an important one to keep in mind in interviewing as in other areas of service. The human service worker is not only an individual, he is also a representative of a particular agency and, in a wider sense, of the society in which the agency functions. The person asking for his help sees him in all these lights even if he is not aware of them. It follows, then, that in the future when he is in need of service, or even if he is able to provide it, previous experience will color his behavior. What is said to him today may be heard for many years to come.

This thought may almost prevent the beginning human service worker from speaking at all for fear of saying the wrong thing. And it is probably wise for a human service worker to be somewhat inhibited about asking questions when this is not a stipulated part of his job. Listening is perhaps even more important than speaking in the human services, and it is in general the less well-developed tool. It is because so few people are really good listeners that many people come to the human services for help. The need to be heard is felt as early as the need to make sounds. Parents and teachers know how many ways children can find to break into adult conversations and turn attention to what they want heard. To be a "voice crying in the wilderness"—to be unheard and misunder-stood—has for thousands of years been recognized as a terrible fate. Even today where there seems to be a superabundance of com-munication, many people suffer from feeling themselves in this lonely position, because from reasons of physical handicap, race, color, age, or class they cannot make their voices heard, or because there is no one who is interested in listening to them.

What is to be gained from listening to another person talk about what is troubling him?—perhaps nothing, or perhaps the heavy burden for the human service worker of learning about problems which he is unable to solve. But this is not a valid objection since human services are intended to increase the well-being of the indi-viduals who seek them, not the one who has chosen to provide them. Some people believe that if a troubled person is not encour-aged to discuss his problems he will the more easily forget them. And there are certainly many times when for one reason or an-other it is not possible or desirable for the human service worker to encourage a troubled person to talk while he remains a silent, at-tentive listener. At the same time, the human service worker needs to be sensitive to another's need to "just talk" about what is on his mind, a kind of talk that does not require the worker to respond with solutions, indeed, to respond at all. What he needs to do is to listen with attention and sympathy. It may help him to do this if he remembers times in his own life when he needed to "talk to someone."

Almost everyone has had some experience with the phenomenon of "talking things out" and finding them more manageable after such a session. No one knows exactly why this is true. It may be related to the complex interaction of thought and language. To put thoughts into words requires a sorting out, an intellectual pro-cedure that imposes a kind of order on the thoughts, fears, appre-hensions, anxieties, and realities that mill about in one's mind. To express anything requires a complicated marshaling activity which assigns priorities, translates feelings into words, and orders words into sentences that will convey meaning. This process in itself separates the most real and pressing concerns from those which are less so. Then even if those concerns are not immediately ex-pressed they are less frightening because they have been examined and organized.

This process goes on almost constantly in every human mind without words actually being spoken. The ability to put feelings and thoughts into language is one of the most significant differences between man and other animals. But it would appear likely that, as man the social animal feels most comfortable when he is with his fellows, so when he is able to share his thoughts with them, to speak and be heard, he feels safer, more protected, stronger.

This is not to suggest that just listening interminably is necessarily the best way of helping people to solve problems. When to listen, when to talk, what to listen for, and how to interpret it are subjects which require special study and training according to the field of service and the kind of responsibility the human service worker is expected to carry. Eventually, some human service workers will need to develop a special ability to listen well and recall what has been said to them and how it has been said, but all human service workers need to remember that a sympathetic listener lightens the speaker's burden and decreases his pain—whether it is a toddler's stubbed toe or an old man's lonely terminal illness—while it gives the worker insights not revealed by direct questions.

In practice, most human service workers find it is easier to listen to people, difficult as this may be at times, than to be met with silence or a baffling "I don't know" answer to questions such as, "Why did this happen?" or "What happened?" The human service worker's job often depends on his success in getting certain kinds of answers so it is not surprising that his failure is upsetting. Then, too, silence or short noncommittal answers are often thin veils over tremendous anger, resentment, and even contempt. The human service worker must not avoid seeing them although it is never pleasant to be the object of such feelings. It is even more upsetting when one has carefully explained the reason for the question and the importance of a full answer. In such instances the worker needs to remember that what he hears himself say may not be what the other person hears. Hearing, like vision, is distorted by the situation. The hearer may be deaf to words spoken in a particular accent, tone of voice, or language. He may be oversensitive to certain sounds uttered in certain surroundings. And he may actually not know the answers to questions because he cannot hear the question for the sounds going on in his own mind or because he may want so much to forget what has happened that he actually cannot recall it.

Very few people, under any circumstances, can say completely honestly why they have taken a particular action. They have acted on messages in a code unknown to them. There are so many involved reasons for every human action that the most anyone can do, in general, is to ascribe it to one or two of those whose meaning is plain. This is not a new phenomenon. People have assigned responsibility for their actions to supernatural forces, to the positions of the stars, to the influences of powerful people, to their own base instincts—or to their nobler ones—since time immemorial.

If human service workers develop their ability to listen they will find that they can "hear" their own, unasked questions, which will permit them to express what they want to say in a way most likely to get an answer.

Whether the human service worker is a newcomer to the field or has had many years of experience, his ability to interview, to hear and respond, to ask questions and listen to answers, and to be unperturbed by stony silence or rambling, seemingly irrelevant discussions will be a constantly useful and necessary tool.

4 | description

Having made observations and learned all he can from talking and listening, the human service worker is likely to be impatient to "do something" to help. Most of the people who are attracted to the human services are active, practical people who find their greatest satisfactions in action rather than in contemplation and theorizing. When help is asked of them, they want to respond as quickly as they can. They may also feel some pressures on them to act from the agency in which they work and from the community itself. But action may not result in much success unless the human service worker takes the time and makes the effort to review for himself what he has seen and heard and attempts to analyze what he now knows, what gaps there are in his knowledge, and how the picture he is able to fit together matches pictures he has seen or learned about in the past.

Even then, he is not quite ready to act. He needs to do more than cast a fleeting glance, noting only that "something is wrong." Rather, he must try to be as precise as possible about what that distortion may be, adjust his view, and plan his future action accordingly. At the same time he must bear in mind that his job is not to change people in accordance with his personal views of the norm, but to help them achieve the greatest degree of satisfaction that they themselves seek. Inevitably, this must be somewhere within the tolerance of society or the individual will be unable to function freely. It may well be that the human service worker's job will include helping society to tolerate the individual. If he is to succeed in either or both cases, the human service worker must take the step which is here called description before he can take further action with a reasonable assurance of success. Description is called "diagnosis and treatment plan" in some professions. In theoretical science it may be designated as "forming a hypothesis." Whatever it is labeled, it is a summing up of all that has been learned about a subject from direct contact. In most human services such learning is done through observation and interviewing. (In medical settings certain physical procedures are likely to be used also.) These findings are then described and matched against previous situations. The human service worker may then reach some tentative decision about what the difficulty may be and so make a plan as to how to help to resolve it.

It is obvious that people with a wealth of life experience or years of specialized training will be more skilled in coming to such decisions than will those with little previous experience. It may be recalled, however, that in the old story about the Emperor's clothes, it was a little boy who noted that the Emperor had no clothes on while the grown-up courtiers, blinded by years of obedient sub-servience permitted themselves to see what they were supposed to see. The beginning worker may, on occasion, have so fresh a view of a human situation that his description of it may be as valuable as that of more experienced staff members. For this reason, many agencies attempt to bring together staff members from a number of levels of experience and training to describe their angle or view on a problem and to work out a joint plan. Each worker can make a contribution to this kind of meeting and will do it most easily and successfully when he has trained himself to do the kind of mental summing up that is called "description."

Human service workers, in their turn, will do well to remember that describing what is seen and heard and acting on this descrip-tion is not a process confined to the human services, but like all the tools used in its formulation, is a natural, everyday procedure car-ried on by the many laymen who have talent for dealing with peo-ple. They, too, are valuable members of the human service team if their expertise is sought and respected.

child care: babysitter

A babysitter said:

> And it was real cute yesterday, instead of the mother telling the boys to be good, the boys looked up and said, "Now, Momma, you be good while you're gone." Instead of her saying that to the boys, they said that to her. I thought that was real, real cute, you know. And they never said a word when she walked out and left them yesterday. They must be used to being walked out and left with somebody. You can generally tell, that when the kids cry, they haven't been left very much, but if a kid has been left with

From *The Day Care Neighbor Service* by Alice H. Collins and Eunice L. Watson (1969), p. 32. Reprinted courtesy of the Tri-County Community Council, Portland, Ore.

> this one and that one and they've gotten so they don't care who they're left with, they don't pay any attention to who they're left with at all. These two kept playing with their toys and never said a word when the mother left and only looked up and said, "Well, Momma, you be good while you're gone."

The babysitter has made use of her observations and conversations in the past to guide her behavior in a new situation. It seems safe to assume that by doing so, she was more able to understand the boys and to ascribe their behavior to past experience rather than to indifference or to any neglect or lack of concern in the mother. She could even plan her own activities better because she recognized that these children would need little of the kind of attention she would have to give to children separated for the first time from their mother, although they might enjoy an outing or special activity that their busy working mother had little time for.

Description, when it is carefully and consciously undertaken, even in an emergency, may show omissions in observation and interviewing which leave the human service worker with so incomplete a picture that if he uses it to guide him, he may find himself adding to rather than diminishing the problem. Or the situation may seem so urgent and so familiar from his past practice that he acts decisively and rapidly and turns to the next emergency, without taking the time to see his mistakes and to learn from them.

marital conflict:
mrs. r.

In the following episode a number of different agencies were involved and presumably, there were several human service workers—the police, a probation officer, a social worker, and staff at the children's home. All of them acted in accordance with their view of the immediate necessity and none of them learned the true story. This story was reported by a research worker who had made friends with people in the crowded city street where the incident occurred and to whom the mother talked freely when everything was over.

The human service workers were involved as a consequence of a fierce and noisy fight in the front yard of a house in the ghetto between a woman and her husband who was apparently too drunk to defend himself. Someone called the police who stopped the fight and took Mrs. R. to the police station where bail was set at forty dollars pending trial in two weeks. This was a very familiar procedure to the court who saw many combatants in family quarrels. Contrary to custom, however, the trip in the police car and the preliminary court proceedings did not lead, as they usually did, to tearful explanations or to a small payment to a bondsman. Mrs. R. did not return sober to her eleven children as might have been expected. Instead, she chose to go to jail for the two weeks before the trial.

Mr. R. worked and made a bare living. If he stayed home to care for the children he risked permanent loss of his job, which would have put this large family on the welfare rolls. Therefore, since the children were all quite young, arrangements had to be made at once for their care. It was probably a social worker at the Public Welfare Department who arranged that they be sent to Junior Village, an institution for neglected and dependent children. A number of responsible human service workers had acted precipitously on what they had seen and heard without checking back to note that there must be some reason for the unusual behavior of Mrs. R. and to then explore what the reason might be.

The following is some of what Mrs. R. told the research worker afterwards about the incident.

You know, I didn't have to stay in jail those two weeks. I could have paid forty dollars for bail and gotten out, but I just kind of felt that I'd stay there for a while, I just thought I'd be better off.

I had seventy-three dollars on me because I had the rent money. One mind told me to pay the bail and the other mind said no. So when they told me I could make one telephone call and asked me who I wanted to call, I told them to just call the rent man and tell him to come and get the rent and I would stay in jail.

The rent man came and got it that Tuesday. I was glad I paid the rent, as we had to have a place to stay when I got out. The only thing that worried me while I was in jail was the children. I worried about them, as they have never been separated from me before. When I got out of jail my husband came for me and asked me if I didn't want to come home and fix something to eat for the children. I told him, "No, I just want to get the children," and I kept right on from the jail out to Junior Village to get them. They had been taken good care of there, but there won't be no more separations. The next separation will just have to be a

From "Life among low-income Negroes" by Hylan Lewis. In *Employment, Race, and Poverty,* ed. Arthur M. Ross and Herbert Hill. (New York: Harcourt, Brace and World, 1967). Used with the kind permission of Harcourt Brace Jovanovich, Inc.

death separation because I know I won't do anything like that again. . . .

I have always treated my husband nice and tried to help him. I also tried to share. When I have worked I have given him money when he needs it. I don't drink and I told him that if he can't control his drinking then he shouldn't drink. I didn't like him out there in the yard acting ugly in front of all the neighbors. . . .

If the human service workers had noted that their observations had been too hasty or too clouded by their own preconceptions, they might also have realized that what they had learned from listening was no different from that which any bystander could hear—a brawl between a husband and wife. Had they carried out their descriptive tasks as human service workers they might have heard the real story from either Mr. or Mrs. R. and have noticed that Mrs. R. was angry and distressed but not drunk and that the whole episode had a great deal of meaning to everyone involved.

No doubt, all the human service workers in touch with this situation made a brief record of it routinely for their own agency files. It takes little imagination to realize that any court appearance or placement away from home would be a matter of record for those involved. But records also have various uses in different settings. In an institution, for example, where there are two and three different workers in charge of a number of patients over a twenty-four-hour period, it is vital that those coming to work know what went on in the immediate past, at least those events that might have bearing on the next eight hours.

In some settings, long periods of time may elapse between contacts with individuals and families so that they may be strangers to the human service worker. If he is able quickly to glean the case history from a previous record, he may be able to spare the client much painful interviewing.

Although few human service workers express much enthusiasm for this aspect of their work, record keeping takes on a somewhat different light if it can be seen as an opportunity for evaluation. Even if he needs only record one line, the human service worker can get into the habit of a quick mental review of what he has seen and heard as a preliminary to making that notation. If the worker's task is to keep a fairly extensive record he may find that rereading it brings to light facets he had not seen before which may give him valuable insights into a problem. Any record will offer the worker an opportunity to check on himself and on his understanding of the situation at the time when he is forming an initial plan. And it will permit him to review the accuracy of his first impression in the light of what he learns from continuing contact.

While it is always hard to admit one's mistakes, human service workers need not avoid situations where this may occur. The complexity of human nature and the endless variety of social experiences any one individual has had—including the human service worker himself—make it inevitable that he will sometimes be wrong and perhaps need to correct an initial impression many times. It is a mark of his professionalism at any level of training that he keep his mind open all the time to the possibility of error on his part and that he be ready to correct his views when he discovers they were not in line with the new reality he perceives.

The process that has been described in this section is a circular one. Signals of distress are received, decoded, and the message acted on, and then the whole process is continually repeated to be sure that the message was correctly received in the first place and that the action taken has relieved the distress that prompted the signal. This may be a very short or a very long procedure, but for human service workers who enjoy facing a difficult task and a demand for continuing self-improvement, it is an endlessly rewarding one.

| part two | *experiences in human service work* |

5 | *the human service worker and children*

It is logical that Part Two, which concerns the experiences of human service workers, should begin with a focus on children. People begin as children, and in this country, the human services made their beginning with services for children more than one hundred years ago.

Some of the children discussed in this chapter live with their own families and some live with other families or in institutions. For the most part, the children are described through the eyes of the human service workers in contact with them although most of the accounts also picture their families and the close interrelationships that exist there.

The settings in which the services are given are described briefly. It must be kept in mind that only a few of the many different settings for children are included here, and that new ways of caring for children are constantly being tried out and older methods sometimes terminated. The same is true of the human service workers. But, it is safe to predict, in the near future there will be more and more opportunities for people with talent and interest. Those with professional training will tend either to act as supervisors and directors or to work with children and their families in a clinical relationship.

Day care for preschool children whose mothers work is one of the human service fields that has changed more in the past twenty-five years than it did in the hundred years before that. It is an example of how changes in the world outside the home—business, industry, politics—affect everyone, bringing into being new kinds of human services and modifying the established ones through changes in the demand for workers and in the way they perform their services.

Day nurseries where little children were cared for during the twelve-hour working day of their mothers were established when women first began to work outside of their homes. At that time, only women who had no alternative went out to work. These were women whose husbands had been killed or incapacitated in the Civil War, were disabled by illness or injury, or for other reasons

41

could not or would not support their families. The families might
have come to the big cities in search of work and found themselves
stranded, away from customary help of relatives; or they might
have been immigrant families, alone in this country. If there was no
one to care for the children at home, the mother had to leave them
alone, consign them to the care of an unpaid neighbor, or tie them
to a machine at work. The kind middle-class women who organized
and supported the first day nurseries to look after these unfortunate
children were firm in their belief that only those who *had* to work
should be permitted to use them. They believed that any woman
who *chose* to leave her children was immoral and they hired staff
to make home visits and hold interviews to be sure this never
happened.

Today, millions of mothers of young children work, whether or
not it is an economic necessity. Business and industry could not
operate without them. Public opinion has changed, too. Where once
it was believed that it was wrong for a woman to work outside her
home unless she was forced to by economic necessity, today the
practice is widely accepted and even expected of women. Nor is
there any reliable evidence that the children of working mothers
are any different from the children of mothers who do not work.
Research to determine just what effect different kinds of care has
on children is so difficult to do that none has yet been completed.
But there is good reason to believe that the most important influences on the development of a little child are his mother and his
immediate family, and the effect these relationships will have on
him is not to be predicted by the amount of time he spends with
them.

Day care programs of all kinds have multiplied in recent years
as more and more women have gone to work—not only young
mothers, but the middle-aged women who were once natural "babysitting grandmothers." There are many different kinds of people
working in day care programs, including teachers, nutritionists,
child care aides, and family day care givers with or without specialized training. There is no doubt that day care programs will
grow but not necessarily in the direction which they have taken in
the past. It is likely that day care will continue to be the subject of
much debate and discussion at governmental funding levels. The
sums of money involved would certainly astonish the founders of
the first nurseries who had a great deal of trouble convincing just
a few contributors that supporting day nurseries would not result
in a breakdown of all standards of feminine conduct.

One result of the increase in working mothers is the development
of a new social custom which most people think of as "babysitting."

It is accurately termed private family day care. In many neighborhoods there are both working mothers of young children and
mothers who for many reasons prefer to stay at home. A natural
system of exchange has grown up in which the mothers at home
often care for one or several children of their working mother
neighbors, thereby earning some money without leaving home.
Sometimes, conditions influence change—working mothers may
stay home for a time and the at-home mothers may go to work.
There are also family day care givers with grown children who take
on the care of little children because they prefer to remain at home
and enjoy children or because they have few marketable skills.

As a result of the widespread use of this kind of care most little
children today have had the experience of being cared for in the
home of another family or having children of another family cared
for in their home. It may be that this is a kind of modern substitute
for the way families gave each other help in earlier times.

Most states have licensing laws which are intended to cover family day care homes as well as large and small group care facilities.
But few states have funds to do more than attempt to assure that
children are cared for under reasonably healthy physical conditions
and are not grossly abused or neglected. Very few states would
claim that the majority of their day care facilities are licensed, or
that only those that are licensed are capable of giving good care.
New ways of helping to assure that the millions of working mothers
can find the kind of day care they want for their children are constantly and urgently being sought. Two new projects are the settings for the vignettes that follow.

*family
day care home:
sylvia carlson*

This record is excerpted from reports and taped interviews held between a professional social worker in a demonstration family day
care service called the Day Care Neighbor Service and a certified
family day care giver.

Sylvia Carlson had four children of her own, two in school and
two preschoolers, Lisa, two, and Joanne, five. Her husband was a
welder. She told the social worker that they were agreed that she
should not go out to work and Mrs. Carlson said she preferred to
have "just plain old stuff" for her household rather than leave her

children to earn the extras. She had very definite ideas about what was good and bad for children and an easy, firm, happy way of dealing with them. The Carlsons lived in an apartment house where there were many families like themselves, and her kitchen seemed always to hold two or three neighbors and their children to whom she gave coffee and good advice and encouragement in a natural, neighborly way. The social worker called on her about once a month and was available if Mrs. Carlson asked her to come in between these regular visits. The account that follows is about the results of such a request.

When the social worker got there, Mrs. Carlson explained that she was worried about Jane Hartley, age four. Mrs. Roberta Hartley had heard of Mrs. Carlson through a mutual friend and had come to see her and ask that she care for Jane. Mr. Hartley had died a year ago in an automobile accident and she had had to go back to work as a secretary. Jane was "too quiet" and cried a lot and needed someone who would understand her. She talked and acted as if her father were still alive.

Mrs. Carlson was already taking care of a three-year-old and did not want to take on another child but she agreed to take Jane until she got acquainted with her and then she would try to find someone else, maybe in the same apartment house, who would take care of her.

Jane was indeed quiet and tearful when she first came, but after a few weeks her behavior swung to the other extreme.

> DAY CARE GIVER: Since Jane, I mean since she's come out of her shell, she's got so extreme that if Roberta doesn't cut down pretty soon, it'll be rough. Because the kid's got so she talks—she's just got exactly the opposite of what she was. I mean she's so . . . you don't know what right now. And she'll kick at her mother and say, "I hate you" and everything! And poor Roberta, it hurts so bad you can just see it. It hurts all over you know. "What'll I do, what'll I do?" And she hasn't got the heart to just spank her, she's been through so much. When she first came this kid worried me because all she'd do was sit in one spot and for no reason at all she'd start crying off and on all day long. Wouldn't eat or anything. Well, in the two weeks I had her, at the end of it, she was going outside and playing with the kids and eating like a little horse. But I told Roberta I just couldn't go on. So I got Sara downstairs to take her. . . . And I told her, you know, the background and everything. So she said, "Let me try it. . . ." She was over here today and I asked her how she

Summarized from an unpublished taped interview. Used with permission.

liked Sara and she said, "Oh, I just love Sara." And I said, "Well, that's good." And she said, "Sara don't give me no trouble." OK, so now I don't know. This is a four-year-old kid talking. But the way she acts around her mother. I know how she acts around her mother, because her mother comes over and visits me. And I don't think she acts like that with Sara, because Sara won't put up with it.

SOCIAL WORKER: Mmmm—well, it may be that this is strictly related to her own upset, what happened to her—

DCG: Well, it's like Roberta says, she doesn't know if it's spoiling her so much and giving in to her so much, you know. It's not helping her. . . .

march 17

Mrs. Carlson called the social worker to talk again about Jane. Sara had refused to care for her any longer so Mrs. Carlson had resumed care, but she found it very difficult because Jane was so "mean" to her mother. The social worker explained that this might be an expression of Jane's unhappiness over the loss of her father, that people sometimes transferred one set of feelings from their original object to another. She suggested that Mrs. Hartley could take Jane to the Child Guidance Clinic and gave Mrs. Carlson the address.

april 18

SW: Yeah, well now, if you want me to call the clinic about Jane and see if we can help pave the way ahead of time, let me know.

DCG: I want to talk to Roberta about this because—well, I kind of put it off, but now—I'm just going to ask her if she just won't go up and have a talk with them, because this with Jane is not right, it's not natural. I mean, she found out that I won't put up with the sassiness and the back talk. Now like today, I whomped her on the bottom and set her in the corner. But boy, when her mother walks through that door you never seen a kid change so fast in your life. I mean, it's not, you know, only the time she starts crying and kissing and—this is natural—I've had my kids do it to me, too. But at night it's, "Mother, I'm going home and you'd just better come on," and yank her, you know. And Roberta will say, "I'm tired, honey, let me have a cup of coffee with Sylvia." "Well, I'm not staying here!"—and Roberta'll give in to her and yet she wants me to make her mind. Well, you can't fool a kid that way. It's going to be one way or the other, and I'm not going to punish my kids when they do wrong and not her 'cause that's not fair to any of them, including her. But like now she's walking around out there by herself. She won't play with anybody. And I've had the kids walk up, I've even told Joanne, "Honey, ask Jane to play with you," and I'll lean over the porch railing and listen to see if Jane does, and she doesn't. "I don't want to play with you!" And as much as pushes Joanne away from her, so I just gave up on that, too.

SW: (looking out the window) Yeah, I can see the kids left her alone. Is that a doll she brings from home?

DCG: Yeah, I thought maybe if she had something of her own —'cause Roberta made her bring three dolls first thing off the bat, to share with the girls because she had to be taught to share. And I thought this was fine. Well, that day she sat on the dolls and hid the dolls and did everything to those dolls, except let Joanne and Lisa have one. Well, Joanne, she just thought to heck with it and she went to play with the other kids. Of course, Lisa is another thing, you can't make her understand this, you know. She sees the dolls and she wants them too. And next morning I told Jane, I said, "Now, honey, you're either going to share the dolls, or put them up." And that's when she went into a screaming fit about hating me, hating this house, didn't like the kids, didn't want to stay here, wasn't going to stay here, and pounding her heels and bawling. Finally, it kind of scared me so I shook her by the shoulders and told her to come off of it. Nobody'd hurt her. And I—she kind of calmed down. Now, when my girls act up, I might pop them on the bottom and send them to the bedroom and say, "when you can act like a little lady and behave yourself you come out." And it's five minutes and here they come. So, I did the same with Jane and she shut right up as soon as I put her in there. And I told her when she quit crying and behaved she could come out. I said, "Jane, you don't have to stay in there. When you quit your crying and be a good girl, come on out," and I took her by the hand and brought her out, you know. But that's the only time she's ever let me touch her. . . . I mean it's just everything is wrong. No matter what you try it isn't the right thing to do. So I think I'm going to ask Roberta, like I said, just ask her to go to the Child Guidance to see if they can't work with her and find out, because it could be she might snap out of it and yet she might not. And Roberta may get mad at me—but—that's a hard thing for a parent, you know.

SW: Well, it is hard and that's why maybe she needs a lot of help. Because maybe Jane is awfully mixed up about her father. Death is a pretty big thing even for grown-ups to get used to and little children sometimes are awfully mixed up about what has happened. People tend to avoid talking to them about it and say confusing things, even like he's just gone away for a while. Then children wait and get pretty discouraged and sometimes they even think it was something they did that keeps the person from coming back, or that he really doesn't love them enough to. Children would be better off if people told them the truth like with Jane, that her father loved her a whole lot, that he didn't want to die and leave her, and that she can love him always— and that it is sad. But that would be awfully hard to say by someone like Roberta who is having her own struggles with her feelings about losing her husband and being so sorry for Jane and all. So maybe someone outside the family could do it more easily and better, and I'm sure the Child Guidance Clinic people—they have different ones, social workers and psychologists and psychiatrists—could decide how best to do it and then go on seeing Roberta and Jane for a while until it straightened out.

may 18

DCG: Well, you know how Jane was? Well, after you left last time I told Roberta about taking her up to the Child Guidance Clinic and finding out what was going on and she said she'd think about it. Then, later, Jane started crying and I took her out in the kitchen. And I said, "Now, Jane, there is something on your mind. You're not hurt, you're not sick, now what is the matter?" Well, first because she couldn't ride her bike, she said. And I said, "Well, honey, you don't have a bike, anyway. What's the matter?" And there was two or three other excuses. And then, all of a sudden, this big blow up—she wants her daddy. So we talked about a half-hour and I remembered sort of what you had said and said it to her and said it was God's will, and her daddy was with God and all. And I must have hit right, because there was no argument. Anyway, she—Oh my God, the change in that girl! Just boom! So Roberta came home, I was telling her, you know. And I don't know, I just—something made me think of it—I don't know what it was—anyway, I said, "What have you got down there that reminds her so much of him?" I said, "You keep it—you keep him alive constantly." And she said, "Well, yes. She wants to set a place at the table and we do."

SW: Had Roberta ever told you what had happened?

DCG: He had an auto accident. Jane was with him when it happened. And anyway, well, I said, "Granted you don't want her to forget him, but you don't want her to go back either. She's going back, she's still talking baby talk, like when her Daddy was alive." And so I told her—she said she had pictures of him out and there was still two dresses that he had bought her and different things, you know. I said, "Roberta, put them away." She looked at me kind of funny and I said, "Yes, put them away." And I said, "For crying out loud, stop putting that place on the table. And start talking new things. When she's older, ten, eleven, twelve—whenever you feel she is old enough to comprehend, and know what it is about, then—" Roberta called me over the other day. She was packing stuff away, and getting rid of a bunch of stuff, and she gave it to me to give to those who needed it. And she said that she had taken all that stuff and packed it away for Jane, and when Jane was older she could have it.

SW: Well, there are two things about this. Jane needs to know the reality, but she also needs to be able to feel sad if she needs to, you know.

DCG: Yeah. I told her that, I had told her in the kitchen, and everything, and I said that she knows that Daddy's dead, and she can't have her daddy back. And, anyway, like I said, somehow during the conversation, anyway—Roberta was going to call you and thank you for letting us do all this you know, because Jane was doing so good. She said, "Boy, I sure appreciate this."

SW: Everything worked out right. How has Jane been with the other kids?

DCG: She's played, and you know, played house with them, and they ride bikes together. Now she doesn't talk baby talk as bad as she used to a couple of weeks ago. . . .

SW: Well, I thought she was quite talkative today.

DCG: And you know how she has been—sit there and not budge. But she's acting more like a five-year-old girl now, you know. Roberta may move when her office moves in a couple of months. . . . She said, "Yeah, but we can come to see you once in a while." And she said, "One thing about it, I'll never forget you for this. You have done so much for Jane." And I said, "No, I just treat her like one of my own. I haven't done anything for her that I wouldn't do for one of my own."

SW: Well, it's, you know, one of the things that happens is that people, when they're at a point of crisis, hear what other people have to say much faster than they do when, just when they're not in a mess of some kind. And so that what you did, it was important.

At first glance, this illustration might be taken as an example of how a professional social worker can influence the development of a child. But a more careful look will show that it is really an illustration of how two human service workers can collaborate to help a family. As a family day care giver Mrs. Carlson heard distress signals she might have been deaf to in her private capacity. Being a keen observer, she noted small differences in Jane's behavior and in that of her mother that suggested the existence of some problems. Interviewing the social worker gave Mrs. Carlson new insights into Jane's behavior and a plan, part conscious and part unconscious, that she put into effect with rapid and gratifying results. Without the help of the social worker, Mrs. Carlson might have had a great deal more difficulty in understanding Jane's behavior and in helping change it. Without Mrs. Carlson's close contact with the family, Jane's difficulties would perhaps not have come to the attention of any professional helping people until she was in school when it would have been much more difficult to help her and her mother. Neither human service worker had invested a great deal of time in this situation but both had the satisfaction of knowing that what they had done together might have a lifelong influence on the lives of others.

day care aide: barbara

Many mothers, living in the most crowded and poor sections of large cities, have been unable to make the kind of arrangement that Mrs. Carlson and Roberta worked out between them. The few jobs open to them by reason of race or education do not pay enough to permit them to pay for good child care. Yet staying at home, dependent on public support—and open to public criticism—prevents them from giving their children anything more than the bleakest necessities with no prospect for making use of personal talents and interests. Some interesting innovative programs have attempted to break this vicious circle in various ways. The following offers some brief glimpses into the life of a young family moving from despair to hope through a publicly supported program.

"I didn't know I would be good at this. I'm just beginning to get a little self-confidence back."

Courtesy of the New York City Human Resources Administration, from the *Annual Report* (New York, 1969), p. 22.

She broke into an instantaneous smile while she went on packing the wicker hamper with sandwiches and toys in the Center's makeshift kitchen; then she pursed her lips in seeming embarrassment at expressing her own sense of worth. The program's directress, watching from the doorway, arms akimbo, said, "She's not good, she's wonderful."

Barbara T. . . . who is 27, black, slender, shyly beautiful, a mother responsible for her own four children and an Education Aide at the Community Life Family Day Care Center headquartered above a church in Harlem's Mt. Morris section, was preparing for her summer morning rounds.

Waiting for her at windows or in tenement doorways would be the young children of other Harlem mothers, children who today would be making their first excursion to the Bronx Zoo. For some it was their first excursion anywhere.

Mrs. T. is part of a complex of services by which the Center, one of 20 such family day care programs funded by HRA, provides daily "living room" care, play, and learning experiences for the young children of welfare mothers. The mothers are then free to pick up their schooling, enter job training and go to work, taking advantage of opportunities located for them by the Center and in some cases dreamed up by it. All kinds of institutions tend to be drawn into the act, from HRA's own manpower services to hospitals that need aides and major department stores that agreed to provide on-the-job training to women as cashiers and seamstresses.

The system sponsors "provider mothers," who don't want to go out into the commercial world but want to care for other women's children in their homes each day. They are glad to undergo the training, meet the standards, enjoy the children, and earn dollars for it. There are "user mothers," many in homes without fathers, who are eager to escape their early, lonely burial at home and to give their children new experiences while they work and get off welfare. And there are education aides like Barbara, who enrich the whole program by going into homes to introduce something of the world to isolated children, or take the children out into the world.

She had started as a provider mother. She unraveled the past while walking along a row of butcher shops lit by the morning sun and bars that opened early, on her way to her first charges. People recognized her and waved her on her way.

"I was born on Long Island. My mother left when I was a kid but my father stood by us. I dropped out of school in tenth grade. When I was 16 I ran away to Mexico, I don't really know why. I married an actor and I had four children. I don't know where he is now, someplace in Europe.

"I worked for a good while as a night waitress in Howard Johnson's but one night—you were always relying on different people—my baby sitter walked out and left my children and my baby alone. That was the end of my working. I went on welfare.

"I stood it as long as I could. Then I heard about this program and I offered to take other people's children into my home. I had my own kids' puzzles and toys and books. Some of those children had never seen a book."

As she turned a corner, a heavy-set woman dressed for work hailed her, and three children, the youngest about four, began trailing after her. When they ran ahead she called "Stop at the corner . . . Edgar, take Bernice's hand."

"A lot of these kids have lived like shut-ins. If the mothers are managing alone, by the time they shop and cook and wash, they don't have a minute to take the children into the park. The children aren't ready for school when the time comes. I had one little girl in my house who had dropped out of kindergarten because there was nobody to take her. After she came to me, why, in no time she was even beginning to read.

"After about six months, Mrs. Marbury, our director, asked me would I like to train as an education aide. God, I was happy. I've seen these kids open up. I've taken them out of their houses whenever I could. They'd never seen a firehouse or the river. We've gone on boat trips to Staten Island, and they've made paper flowers, and told me how they feel at night. . . .

"Me? Mrs. Marbury says I've got it in me to be a teacher. I'm working toward my high school equivalency. The part of the exam I took—well, I scored 12th grade. But the math, I'm afraid of it.

"You know, having to be on welfare takes so much out of you. I'm just trying to get some self-confidence to go on. Maybe someday I'll get to college and be a teacher. I want to . . . I don't know. . . ."

She walked erect. She let the smile come back. Then she disappeared into the subway with the children, bound for the zoo, which she herself had never visited as a child.

As the native skill and intelligence of people like Barbara and the handicaps she suffered from dropping out of school have become recognized, the educational system has come under increasing consideration. Why do some children make so little use of the many hours of school provided for them? How much responsibility

should teachers be expected to take for the development of the "whole child," since teachers are a part of the everyday lives of all American children over a long period of time during their most impressionable years? Should teachers teach subjects or children? And assuming that the answer is some of both, how do they do this? Many systems of education have been tried, and there is agreement only that no one way of teaching will succeed with all children, and therefore that education must be flexible and responsive to the talents and needs of children whose family, social, and ethnic backgrounds vary greatly. This is a goal that is only now being more or less widely accepted, and no one is as yet ready to describe the steps to be taken to reach it. Certainly, some steps have been taken already; some educators do recognize differences between pupils, not in terms of academic achievement alone, but positively, in terms of potential and challenge.

In the following article a teacher talks frankly about his pupils in a way he might not have done a few years ago.

ghetto school: elementary teacher

When a child of 6 or 7 from the ghetto meets up with the politics of the street or the schoolyard, he brings along both the sensual and the fearfully moral experience he has had at home. Slum children live at close quarters to their parents and their brothers or sisters. They are often allowed to be very much on their own, very free and active, yet they are also punished with a vengeance when distracted or forlorn parents suddenly find an issue forced, a confrontation inevitable. They face an ironic mixture of indulgence and fierce curtailment.

Such children come to school prepared to be active, vigorous, perhaps much more outgoing on an average than middle-class children. But they are quick to lose patience, sulk, and feel wronged and cheated by a world they have already found to be impossible, uncertain, and contradictory. Here are the words of an elementary-school teacher who has worked in a northern ghetto for 3 years and still feels able to talk about the experience with hope as well as bitter irony:

Courtesy of Robert Coles, "Violence in Ghetto Children," Children 14 (May-June, 1967): 103.

"They're hard to take, these kids, because they're not what you think when you first come, but they're not what you'd like for them to be either. (I don't mean what I used to like for them to be, but what I want for them now.) They're fast and clever, and full of life. That was the hardest thing for me to realize—that a boy or girl in the ghetto isn't a hopeless case, or someone who is already a delinquent when he comes into the first grade. The misconceptions we have in the suburbs are fantastic, really, as I think back—and remember what I used to think myself.

"I expected to find children who had given up, and were on the way to fail, or to take dope, or something like that. Instead it was in a lot of ways a breath of fresh air, talking with them and teaching them. They were friendlier, and they got along better with one another. I didn't have to spend half the year trying to encourage the children to be less competitive with one another. We don't call middle-class children "culturally deprived," but sometimes I wonder. They're so nervous and worried about everything they say—what it will mean, or what it will cost them, or how it will be interpreted. That's what they've learned at home, and that's why a lot of them are tense kids, and even worse, stale kids, with frowns on their faces at ages 6 or 7.

"Not a lot of the kids I teach now. They're lively and active, so active I don't know how to keep up with them. They're not active learners, at least learners of the knowledge I'm trying to sell them, but they're active and they learn a lot about the world, about one another. In fact, one of the big adjustments I've had to make is realizing that these kids learn a lot from one another. They are smart about things my kids will never understand. They just don't think school is worth a damn. To them it's part of a big outside world that has a grip on them, and won't let them get any place, no matter how hard they try. So what's the use, they ask themselves; and the answer is that there isn't any use—so they go right on marking time in class until they can get out.

"We teachers then figure they're stupid, or they're hopelessly tough and "delinquent," or their homes are so bad they'll always be "antisocial" or "incorrigible." I've found that when they're playing and don't know I'm looking they are different kids—spontaneous, shrewd, very smart, and perceptive. Then we go back into the classroom, and it's as though a dense fog has settled in on all of us. They give me a dazed look, or a stubborn, uncooperative one, and they just don't do anything, unless forced to—by being pushed and shoved and made to fear the authority they know I have."

Schools in many cities have begun to recognize the need for new ways of teaching the children who, feeling as the teacher has described, learn almost nothing and, at the same time, disrupt the class to the point where other children cannot learn either. Various approaches are being tried to solve this problem now although the most thoughtful educators recognize that much must be done in the future to bring pupils and teachers into the relationship that fosters real learning.

special
learning project:
teacher's aide

One attempt to reach the most disruptive students is described by
a college student, who dropped out to get some experience with
"real life."

I was a teacher's aide in a SLD program—special learning difficulties—instead of going to college my junior year.

There were forty-two kids and they were supposedly all disturbed, but it turned out that some were a lot more than disturbed
and some were just discipline problems. Other schools sent
them. This place had a long waiting list—there were six kids to
a class—six to eight kids and a teacher and an aide.

I had a whole list of things that I was supposed to do—like
take all the kids out to recess, take attendance and all that, have
them all orderly when the teacher arrived, and then do anything
the teacher told me to do. One teacher wouldn't let me do anything and one teacher let me do a lot.

If the first teacher was doing something and one kid was acting up, I was supposed to calm him down or take him out of the
room. That teacher was boss—she was the head of everything
and she was constantly trying to make the kids aware of that.
She had a really hard class—they were all black except for one
white boy and he was really mean. She was really scared of the
kids—there were 12 of them—tough and big and calling her all
these names. She was Jewish and they held that against her—
called her beak nose. They started liking me in the beginning
—they thought I was a lot of fun—but then she used to do
things to put me down in front of the kids and then they'd all
say, "Miss P got burned, Miss P got burned!" Then they lost all
their respect—it was amazing. I got really scared in that class;
I couldn't imagine myself trying to stand up and control them
like that teacher did. In order to control them she'd have favors
in her hands. She'd say, "Now if you'll be quiet you'll get one of
these," and every day she'd have something different. And then
they'd get all excited and she'd say it was my fault. She never
really talked to me about what it was all about. She told me I
was inferior to her and she wanted me to listen to her and not to

From an unpublished taped interview.

get carried away by the kids. She was just a teacher without special training—she got fired after that year.

In the afternoon I went to another teacher. His kids were easier to handle but he was a lot better to them, too. He was sort of a father image to them. He'd hit the kids which he wasn't supposed to do but it kept them in line. Some of those kids, you know, you just felt like—he'd slap them and it would sort of get them back into the world or something. His classroom was really orderly—when he said for it to be quiet it was quiet, and the kids would get in their seats and get their books out. It was impressive to look at. He gave me two kids that were doing real well and he told me I should work with them—they were going to regular school next year. So I did a lot of reading with them— got really close to them—they were really good kids. But the rest of the class was wild and they would get lured by them sometimes.

I think I might like to work with kids like that but I'd want to do what I wanted to do myself. I think I'd like to work with them in small numbers—like one or two is a lot better than a class.

day nursery: handicapped child

The short vignette that follows describes an episode in a nursery school operated in conjunction with an institution for mentally retarded children.

Little children who have crippling physical handicaps which will prevent their normal development move most adults to the deepest sympathy and a wish to "make it up to them" somehow. Since that is not really possible, they often treat such children in especially indulgent ways as a means of compensating them for their tragic lacks. But such indulgence may emphasize for the children that they are different from others. It may lead to behavior that separates them even more from rewarding relationships with their peers or adults. On the other hand, strict discipline and standards of behavior impossible for them to reach may bring them into greater despair and frustration with their inadequacies.

People with great native patience and a capacity for seeing the suffering child behind a sometimes grotesque exterior need much training in order to be prepared to guide the educational and socializing program necessary for severely handicapped children.

Many interested and gifted assistants are needed because these children sometimes require individual care, especially when they are very young.

The little girl described here was living in her own home and attending a day nursery. She was taught by a highly trained educator who knew how to help this handicapped child to form a human relationship that would be the key to her future.

She came into our Day-Care a fiery-haired five-year-old with a temper the same shade. Cerebral palsied, and unable to talk, she lashed out at an unfair world with an unspeakable fury. Torn by the mixed emotions of her parents who had alternately spoiled and disciplined her, this extremely sensitive child seemed beyond control when she entered our little group. The hurricane raged for several weeks while I probed all the recesses of my mind to find the eye of the storm. We learned to duck with agility all that she threw, to keep a level head, and to follow, with the strictest adherence, a routine designed for the comfort and growth of all the children. We ignored her nonconformities. Her actions, for all intents and purposes, were not getting through to me. Furthermore, they were not impressing her classmates.

All this time she watched me. She wanted me to be angry too for this was her trick in trade. Oh how I wanted to spank her for her tirades and inconsiderations but I did not because this procedure would be old hat to her.

One day I was particularly tired and discouraged and she must have sensed something amiss. Spilling milk is not unusual in a pre-school situation, but our little firebrand made a last stand. She threw her milk at me with deadly accuracy. I sat stunned for a minute. As the milk dripped from my hair, I deliberated—one false move could undo everything. I felt an angry tear in my eye. She looked at me, her face red and contorted with emotion. I didn't move. Suddenly, she staggered from the room. Still I sat, knowing I must take some action. A few moments passed. She came running back into the room, hands dripping with wet paper towels. I didn't move. . . . She smoothed back my hair and wiped my face and clothes with erratic, awkward hands. She had suddenly dissolved into a compassion she failed to comprehend because she had never needed it; it was a brand new experience. Involuntarily my arms went out and she flew in.

From "The Promised Land" by Burton Blatt et al. In *Christmas in Purgatory* (Boston: Allyn and Bacon, 1966), p. 77. Reprinted with the kind permission of the publisher.

It is a mark of the high degree of skill and training of this nursery educator that she recognized her natural angry reaction to the thrown milk but could *act* on her professional understanding of the reasons behind the action of the child. She could thus uncode a message totally incomprehensible to the sender and send a silent, but well-understood reply.

One of the things that makes work with young children satisfying to the human service worker is that when he is able to offer some help, he can often see things change for the better quite quickly. He then can enjoy the knowledge that he has made a contribution toward another person's well-being.

Every human service worker needs this kind of experience to offset the anguish of the opposite kind. Undoubtedly he will find himself face to face with people who badly need and want his help, but whom he is powerless to help because their problem is created by the social conditions under which they are forced to live. Millions of people in this country today suffer from deprivation and neglect through no fault of their own. Human service workers who have chosen to try to help the people who need them have frequent contact with such individuals and often feel desperate over their own inability to correct the conditions which cause the problems.

It is in no case quick, easy, or simple to change social conditions which are well established by tradition and reinforced by ignorance—real or simulated—of the true facts. But even though a great deal remains to be done, there have been some changes in national attitudes toward destructive conditions and more can be foreseen if human service workers bear in mind that their task is not just to help individuals or help them to adjust to an intolerable life, but to use what they know to help change those conditions or support the efforts of their clientele to help themselves through social action.

indian reservation: flap and loueena

The following scenes from a novel about a southwestern Indian reservation allow only glimpses of the human service worker—a public health nurse—but give a graphic picture of the conditions under which she worked. It is safe to assume that she was distressed with the lack of health services that existed on the reservation and the living conditions which not only were conducive to illness and death but prevented adults from using those services that were available. Possibly she could have helped change these conditions by bringing them persistently to the attention of the government agency which might need such evidence to gain increased public support. She might have allied herself with others on the side of the angry and frustrated Indians in actions described in the other chapters of the book to bring about the changes they wanted. On the other hand, the nurse might well have argued that if she spent her time on community action she would be neglecting patients crucially in need of her professional services and that she was forced to choose to do what she was trained to do. Most human service workers find themselves having to make such difficult decisions in the course of their careers.

The narrator in the following is a young man growing up on the reservation. Flap, the main character in the novel from which these excerpts about a family tragedy were taken, is a much-decorated hero of World War II. He has returned to the reservation and is filled with rage at the government he has served because it has robbed his people of their birthright and is unresponsive to the life and death needs of their children.

In this excerpt one recognizes a human way of dealing with helpless anger that arises from the best of human motives. Flap lists all the people he can think of who have victimized others, because he is so ashamed at his own powerlessness. One can see, too, how his rage comes from his deep love and concern for his friends and how their love for each other provides them with some mutual comfort and strength.

> The door [to the store, called The Place] opened now, and Luke Wolf came in carrying his daughter Loueena. He showed the worry he felt. And Loueena, who was small for ten, looked even smaller and paler than usual, wrapped up in Luke's threadbare old navy peacoat.
>
> Luke forced a grin at Mr. Storekeep. "Well, I guess I'll just have t' sue that there bulldozin' fella. Noise is s' bad it's kept m' little Loueena from sleepin' two nights in a row."
>
> Mr. Storekeep said, "Ya want some more a' them aspirin tablets?"
>
> Flap and I walked over to Luke, me a little unsteady on my feet.
>
> Luke said hesitantly, "—Ain't ya got somethin'—maybe stronger'n that, Mr. Storekeep?—She really ain't feelin' too fine."

From *Nobody Loves a Drunken Indian* by Clair Huffaker (New York: David McKay Co.), pp. 20–25, 46, 157, 220. Copyright © by Clair Huffaker. Reprinted with the permission of the publisher.

Mr. Storekeep fussed around the section of shelf where he kept things that were more or less medicinal. "Just—Vicks Rub, Ex-Lax, iodine, Listerine, Tampax and some Band-Aids."

Flap reached out and pushed some hair back on Loueena's forehead, out of her eyes. She looked up at him and managed a small grin. "Hey, Uncle Flap."

He returned the grin. "Not feelin' too hot, huh?"

Then the hurt came over her again, and she closed her eyes and lips tightly against it. Luke's wife came in and said, "I got the fire built up t' warm 'er. I'll take 'er now."

"I'll be along shortly with the tin a' aspirin," Luke said.

His wife took Loueena. "I got some rocks heatin', too. They'll help keep the cold off 'er." She went out, crooning to the now slightly shaking little girl as she carried her.

Mr. Storekeep scratched his head. "Ya think old Singlefoot Dancer could help 'er?"

Luke shook his head with finality. "No Medicine Man ain't gonna mess aroun' with my Loueena."

"Luke?" Flap asked. "How long's it been since the Bureau doctor was by?"

"Two, three weeks. You know how busy he is."

"Her forehead's hotter'n a pistol."

"—Ya think she's real sick?"

"I'd say she's a little too sick for aspirins."

Luke wet his lips nervously and nodded. "I'll go see if I can't get a doctor on the phone."

Since the nearest telephone was at the Indian Bureau Headquarters, this meant a twelve-mile trip. And Bill Shorthorse had already left in his pickup.

Flap turned to Too Far Williams. "Can he use your horse?"

Too Far said, "Sure," and Luke hurried out. We could hear him riding away at a quick pace that turned into a lope.

Too Far mumbled. "Hope he don't try t' lope it all th' whole way. He'll worsen that horse's saddlesores." . . .

"Don't worry about Loueena," I said. "She'll be all right."

"I'm *not* worried about her!" Flap said, but I still knew he was ."I'm just generally pissed off at everything in general!"

Too Far blinked slowly, thoughtfully. "—Like what?"

Flap stared at him with a brief, deceptively calm expression. "Well, Too Far, I'm pissed off at the ol' Romans for feedin' Christians to the lions. —I'm pissed off at the Christians for burnin' all them people on poles."

"Stakes," I said.

"Steaks my ass, they burned real people!" he said, getting

madder and madder at his black, hopscotch flow of thoughts. "I'm pissed off at the Nazis for killing all them poor goddamned Jews, and I'm pissed off at the Russians for raping all the Nazi girls in Berlin! I'm pissed off at those Chinamen in China for not stayin' good guys, like they were in World War Two! I'm pissed off at Commies an' Phoenix bartenders an' TV! An' I'm pissed off at the United States Cavalry for the goddamned Sand Creek Massacre!"

"Hell," Dick said, "that was eighty years ago."

"That's what I'm talking about! *Historical fact!*" Flap refilled his glass with the "Napoleon Brandy." "An' the thing I'm pissed offest about is that in this day and age a goddamned fella has t' ride a goddamned horse twelve goddamned miles t' make a goddamned emergency phone call about a sick little kid!"

"That ain't so bad," Too Far said. "Few years ago, he'd a' had t' ride clean in t' Phoenix."

Flap glared at Too Far. "Are you sayin' Luke's lucky it's only twelve miles?"

Too Far blinked slowly again, "Well—it's better'n—"

"*And you!*" Flap snarled with fierce contempt. "I'm pissed off at you and every other milk-and-toast 'good' Indian on every reservation in the country!"

Too Far, in addition to being pretty stoned, was surprised and unnerved. "Jesus Christ! What'd I do?"

"*Nothin'!*" Flap stood up so abruptly he knocked the chair over behind him. . . .

"And if Loueena dies, I just may break your neck!"

Too Far was scared, because when Flap's sore, he's got eyes like a mad mountain lion. You know damn well he'll tackle anyone or anything that God ever made.

Too Far gulped and said, "Geez, Flap! That's bein'—loco!"

"Is it?" . . .

[A few days later.]

At The Place there wasn't anyone around, not even any horses or pickups out front. On an impulse, I crossed the dusty space to Luke Wolf's house.

"Hey—Luke?"

He pulled back the Pillsbury Flour curtains on the window to look out. "Come on in, Eleven."

He'd been up long enough to carve a green-willow whistle for Loueena, the kind he'd make as presents for the kids, sometimes, with a hard pea inside of it so that it gave a sweet, warbling whistle when she blew on it. And her mother had made her a pretty toy doll out of a paper sack.

She seemed to be feeling better. She said, "Hey, Eleven," from where she was blanketed up on the dirt floor near the still-glowing coals in the fireplace.

"Hey, yourself."

"Listen." She blew on the musical whistle a couple of times, her breath soft and weak.

"That's real nice," I said.

"That's enough playin' now, honey," Luke said. "You best sleep."

She grinned her appreciation up at Flap and then, with the whistle held firmly in one small hand, she closed her eyes to rest.

Her mother knelt on the ground beside her to tuck the blankets closer around her, and Flap and Luke crossed the room to the other side of the house, where I was standing.

Luke explained that he hadn't been able to get the Bureau doctor because he was off at the Maricopa reservation where they were having some kind of an outbreak, maybe diphtheria.

"But this nurse, a real fine woman, she come an' looked at Loueena." Luke sounded relieved. "Give me some special pills, says Loueena'll be okay. And Loueena slept good after the bulldozer noise finally stopped."

Flap said, "We sure are glad." . . .

Luke Wolf walked in (to The Place) looking like he'd just caught a flying hoof in the pit of his stomach.

"What's the matter?" Flap asked him.

Luke tried to shrug a little, but it didn't quite come off. "—Loueena."

"What about 'er?" Flap frowned.

"They taken 'er over t' the Indian hospital over t' the Salt River Reservation." He cleared his throat. "That nurse lady come an' said Loueena was worse. But not t' worry. She don't think it's too serious."

"Well," Mr. Storekeep said, "they got some real fine facilities over there."

"What seemed t' be wrong with 'er?" Flap asked quietly.

"Dunno. Like—for one thing she didn't even feel like blowin' that whistle ya made for 'er. Just too darn tired, mostly. Her mother went with 'er. An' it's still okay if you fellas wanna watch that TV show later."

"Maybe you'd ruther us not?" Mr. Storekeep said.

"Hell no, I can use the company." Luke grinned at us in a half-hearted way. "See ya later."

When Luke had gone out, Dick said to Mr. Storekeep, "That was a nice thing you said to cheer 'im up."

"About the hospital? Yeah, guess it ain't the best one ever was."

"It's a goddamn half-assed, drafty old Army barracks!" Flap said angrily.

Mr. Storekeeper said, "But—they'll fix her up all right."

Flap said grimly, half to himself, "—They better." . . .

Several days later Luke and his wife were seated in the two chairs, facing the blank television set, their faces drawn and waxlike. Ann Looking Deer was kneeling at the fireplace heating some food for them. . . .

Luke slowly turned his expressionless face toward us. Seeing Flap, he said in a small, lifeless voice, "Hey, Flap."

Flap walked over to behind their chairs and gently put one hand on each of their shoulders. Luke's wife didn't look up, but she raised her hand and laid it on Flap's, their feelings flowing between them through the softly touching hands. Luke did look up. And after a moment he said, "Pneumonia."

Flap nodded, wordless.

Luke swallowed slightly so he could talk again. "They—didn't know. Jus'—nothing—nobody could do."

Flap walked to the wall where the whistle he'd made Loueena was hanging. He touched it, seeing Loueena blowing it and laughing.

It is clear from the foregoing examples that many families, even under conditions of great economic and social deprivation, give their children a home climate in which they can develop and grow. The great majority of families at every level of society can and do act in this way. But there are some who for many reasons and at every socioeconomic level are unable to do so. And illness and death have left some children without immediate families to care for them.

For a good many years it has been held that children in these circumstances should not be deprived of family life but should be provided with a foster home. Such settings are the closest substitutes for their own homes, allowing children contacts with foster parents, sisters and brothers, and other relatives which are believed to be the best basis for normal emotional development. Many agencies which were organized in the last century as orphanages have gradually phased out these group facilities and devoted their efforts to finding and maintaining good foster homes for children in need of them. At the same time, they offer services to the natural parents in the hope that children may eventually return to their own homes.

Although it might appear that the human service worker who finds a child a foster home much superior to his own would have few further problems to deal with, this is not usually the case. Children who have had the kind of unhappy experiences that lead to foster placement do not easily settle into happy relationships with foster parents. And foster parents, interested in taking children into their homes for the nominal sums paid for their care, want the gratification of the affection of the child and the pleasure of seeing him develop under their good care.

As has happened in other fields of human service, it has become increasingly clear that in foster care many different kinds of human service workers may make a contribution, especially in helping the child in his difficult adjustment. Some agencies use case aides in addition to professional staff of various kinds. Though the case aide may be principally occupied in rather routine tasks (taking a child shopping or to the dentist or doctor) he may be able to become the confidant of a troubled child in the way in which a cousin or other relative was likely to do when large families offered their members a variety of personalities and ages from which to choose a "favorite."

foster care agency: college student

The first job I had was at a Foster Child Association in New York. I picked it from a list of jobs at the college I go to that helps students find summer work. I come from the Middle West and I'd never been to the big city. I wanted to be involved with little kids—I don't know why—maybe because I never had any around—I was the youngest. I sort of wanted to find out if I really wanted to be or if it was just a sort of pipe dream.

The place is a real respectable, well-funded agency which used to be a black orphanage. All the students that had been there before mentioned Mr. S. who would be my boss—a wonderful,

From an unpublished taped interview.

paternal, grandfatherly black man who would be great to know—so I looked forward to meeting him.

I met Mr. S. the first morning. I had debated whether I should wear a tie or not and I thought, if they don't say anything then I'll never have to wear a tie and if they do I can always say I didn't know better so I wasn't wearing a tie. So Mr. S. said, "I don't go along with this too much but we're a private agency and we depend on a lot of people for our money and if they come in and see a lot of hippies then we'd lose our money so there is this image we have to put forward so wear a tie." I just had a mustache and medium length hair—and I never had much in the way of good clothes so I was kind of weather beaten but he didn't say anything about that—then. It didn't matter to me to wear a tie—it's just physically uncomfortable. So he introduced me to people and that was nice. I'd never known any black people, really, and here everybody except me was black.

I was nineteen—it just paid enough to live on. I had been told there was very little paper work and lots of contact with kids but it turned out that my contact was mostly just to go out and bring the kids in to see the psychiatrist—either the ones who wouldn't come if no one went to get them or the ones that were too young to come by themselves. In the meantime one of the things I did was to consolidate the files that were really very old. I sort of summed them up on a two-page form.

I had to write a report too of everything that happened when I was with the kids. I didn't mind writing it but I'd get advice I didn't like. "You shouldn't let a seven-year-old walk along the benches in Central Park and pretend he's Batman because that encourages his fantasies." And, "You shouldn't buy them things because they'll exploit you." So finally I just quit writing it down. I did find out that summer that I liked working with kids but I realized I had a lot to learn like, well—I was getting a lot out of the kids but I didn't think they benefited a lot from me. The only reason they did was because I could let them be a lot closer than the older people.

I had a girl—a thirteen-year-old girl who was pregnant—who was so afraid of being pregnant that she wouldn't believe the doctor or the case worker that she was pregnant. She lived with a retired couple. She hadn't been moved around much but they were all through with her now. They felt they'd brought her up just like one of their own and this is how she had rewarded them.

I don't know why she started talking to me in the subway but she did. "I want to marry this guy and I'm going to have his baby and I don't want to tell anybody and I'm only thirteen—and I don't think he wants to marry me and I don't know how to make him want to marry me—and I'm just real scared." She just broke down and fell apart. And I didn't know what to tell her. I couldn't tell her that I thought she was in a bad shape and that the world didn't treat thirteen-year-old girls who were pregnant very well and there was no way with her being a ward of the court that she could marry this guy or keep the baby. She was determined that she was going to keep this baby that she hadn't even told anyone else that she had but she had obviously been racking her mind for the past two months and she had tried to run away a few times, too. I just didn't know how to deal with it. That was about the biggest confrontation that I had. I had a lot of lesser situations, too.

It is likely that the student would have been able to find a job that was easier than foster care aide and one that might have paid him more than board and room. But he probably had no regrets about his choice, though his summer had not been an easy one. He had had the opportunity of learning a good deal not only about the human services but about himself and his own interest and aptitude for this field of work. Summer jobs which offer such try-out experiences are profitable to the students as well as those they serve. Firsthand acquaintance with the people to be met—staff and clientele alike—and with their organizations and customs will bring to life much of what is discussed in theory in classrooms. And no matter what kind of work the student eventually undertakes, his experience with the human service field is likely to enhance his value as a citizen, able to make informed judgments on the issues of his day.

The case aide recognized that he needed to know more if he were to be as helpful to the young unmarried mother as he wished to be, and he could, if he decided to do so, learn more about the tools he needed. But even the most highly trained human service workers are sometimes confronted with human problems which they do not know how to help change. This is quite generally known in the medical services. While human service workers in hospitals or in outpatient facilities find it hard to accept their own ineffectiveness in the face of physical suffering, they have the support of their colleagues and a general public acceptance that there is as yet no known cure for many human ills. In other fields of human service it is sometimes more difficult for the worker to make peace with his own inability to help bring about change in the person and his environment so that he may look forward to a better future.

To some degree, he and others may have unrealistic expectations of what he can accomplish, given the complexity of human lives and the limited knowledge base of behavioral science. It is tremendously frustrating to a conscientious human service worker to find himself faced with a human problem which appears insoluble, and it is especially hard when the problem involves a child whose future is darkly shadowed by present events. Human service workers concerned with protective services and foster care face such problems frequently in their practice. The questions they have to ask themselves are often unanswerable. Is the child likely to be more harmed by being neglected by a parent than by being removed from his own home and placed with strangers? Where can foster parents be found who wish to take on the responsibility of caring twenty-four hours a day for a child who has already learned that adults are untrustworthy and that it is best to grab what one can in an ungenerous world? Will a child who cannot get along in a foster home adjust to a treatment center where he will have to share the adults with other children? And where will he go when he leaves the treatment center—back to his parents? into a new foster care situation?

One of the most trying aspects of this kind of decision making for the human service worker is that he receives messages from so many sources and that they are often contradictory. Parents, in general, want to be good parents though they may, emotionally, be children themselves. Children want to stay with their parents and at the same time want those parents to be what they cannot be. Or they may want to leave their own parents and find others which match their dreams of what parents and home should be like. And having found them, they then often begin to yearn for what they have known before. Human service workers in the schools and courts and the public at large may also make their voices heard.

It is not surprising that sometimes harried workers look for a scapegoat on whom to blame this conflict-ridden situation which, they know, may result in irreversible emotional damage to a child. That scapegoat is likely to be the child's own parents whose failure is responsible for the child's problems—and the workers' sense of professional failure. However, it is more useful for the human service worker to remind himself that neglectful or otherwise inadequate parents are, like everyone else, the result of the interaction between their own natural endowment and the environment in which they have grown up; that there is every reason to believe that they would like to be good parents if they could be; and that fixing blame is a poor substitute for picking up the pieces—or even admitting defeat. The descriptive step discussed in Chapter four can be most useful here. The human service worker, having at the outset made a conscious decision on a plan of action on the basis of observation and interviewing, can now look back to see how it matches what actually has happened. He can assess what part he played in the outcome and try to evaluate how it might have been done differently. If he discovers his errors, he can correct them in the next similar situation he finds himself in, and if he notes that there is as yet no better solution to be found than the one he tried, he knows that he has done all that was possible, and he can seek new ways of dealing with similar problems. In either case, his painful experience will not be wasted and he will be enabled to go on to the next tough one with hope and enthusiasm.

public welfare children's service: harold

There were a number of different human service workers involved with Harold and his family described in the following application to a residential treatment home. Since the family of Harold's mother had long been known to the public welfare agency, it is likely that there had been a succession of workers from that setting who had known the family and had tried to assure them some financial support while attempting to change their way of life to a happier and more independently productive one. Harold's mother, evidently recognizing her inability to play the role of wife and mother adequately, had gone to a mental hospital seeking help. The staff there had been prevented by legal definitions from even trying to provide it. A vocational counselor offered her job training appropriate to her potential as determined by testing and counseling, but she did not finish the course.

The court workers had investigated and made Harold a ward of the court. He had been in a number of schools with a number of teachers and had individual help from a school social worker as well. Harold's father, too, had had some contact with human service workers, professional and volunteer, and had made good use of help. Perhaps Harold's stepmother had been helped to understand the failure of her first marriage and the way to achieve a successful one. Yet honest appraisal of the past, of all that has transpired in his short life combined with the particular talents and needs of Harold at the time of application, would not lead to a very hopeful prognosis for his future. It is not possible to know what his special inborn talents and needs are except that he appears to be a child who has a capacity for using his imagination and reacting rapidly to his environment. But it is possible to see how many adjustments have been required of him and how each one has made the next more fraught with danger and difficulties. No one is to "blame"—but neither has anyone really been able to help. The human service workers who will have contact in the future with Harold may, of course, find that the residential treatment center has been able to reverse the downward trend.* But even after a period of residence, all the human service workers involved with Harold may have to face the sad fact that as yet, no one has really known how to help him to a happier life or how to prevent the difficulties that have beset him.

application for admission to the residential treatment center for harold

the problem

Harold, eleven, is the oldest of three children. His parents divorced when he was three. His mother remarried two years later but separated from her husband. She left the children with her mother and visited irregularly. Responding to the complaints of neighbors, the Protective Services Division of Public Welfare found the grandmother neglectful in her care of the children and living with a series of men. The children were removed from the home and made wards of the court and placed in foster homes. Harold's two younger sisters have remained in the first foster home in which they were placed but he has been moved eight times in the past four years. He is becoming increasingly unhappy, hard to manage and destructive and unless he can be given intensive care it is feared he will be in danger of becoming delinquent or psychotic.

family history

Harold's mother has been known to the welfare agency since she was included in her mother's Aid to Dependent Children grant

From an unpublished case record.

*The community he lives in fortunately has a residential treatment center. Such facilities are so expensive because they need a large, well-trained staff, that there are comparatively few of them and these often have long waiting lists.

in the early 1930s. Her own family background is very unstable and she spent a great deal of time in the Children's Orphanage. During her adult life, she has been erratic and undependable, never assuming the care of her three children for any length of time and often leaving them in her mother's home while she left the state, or lived with men she met in bars.

Two years ago she attempted to commit herself to the state hospital but was not admitted because she was not insane. She was referred to the Division of Vocational Rehabilitation, but half way through the program she became disinterested and did not finish her training. She talks of re-establishing a home for her children, but has never seemed to be able to mobilize herself to do this.

Harold's father was an alcoholic. When he and Harold's mother were living together, he was drinking quite heavily and would often show violent behavior. Since that time, he has been active in Alcoholics Anonymous and has controlled his drinking completely. He has developed a great deal of insight into his own problems and is eager to do what he can for the children. He works consistently and contributes to their support. He is especially fond of Harold and will cooperate as best he can in whatever plans we feel are best for the boy. Last February, he married a divorcee with three children.

Harold's stepmother initially showed a great deal of interest in him. Last fall Harold spent one or two weekends a month with his father and stepmother on visits from his foster home. Because we felt that the marriage was stable and that they could provide an adequate home for Harold, he moved into his father's home during the winter. Harold's initial adjustment was fair. However, Harold felt resentment toward his stepmother and, in order to get attention and affection, began to misbehave. Harold was loud and boisterous around the home; he was slow in doing any of his small jobs, such as drying dishes; he continued to be a "bully" and did not get along well with the children in the neighborhood; he was careless in the home and was destructive of the household furniture and his clothes. The most irritating habit to his stepmother was his incessant lying. It became necessary to remove Harold from the home of his father and place him in another foster home. His stepmother recognizes that she resents Harold's behavior. She experienced one failure in marriage and saw its effect on her three children. While Harold was in the home, tension arose between her and Harold's father and among the children. She is a rather nervous person and could not tolerate the idea that there was a chance that this marriage could also be ruined. She projected the whole blame on Harold. However, she does have many strengths and through counseling, she might be helped to accept Harold.

the child

Although the quality of understanding and the amount of time the various foster parents were able to spend with Harold differed in all of the homes, the child has continued to show similar problems in each placement. At the present time we feel that Harold demands more in patience, understanding and love than a foster home is able to give. The numerous moves have probably interfered with his ability to form meaningful relations with any person for a sustained period of time. Because so many people have disciplined him and expected things of him, Harold does not know what kind of behavior is expected of him. Although there have been different reasons for the different foster parents to request his removal, the reason can almost always be narrowed down to the fact that Harold causes tension in the home and that he is unable to get along with other children in the family and in the community.

At the present time, Harold's problems can be summarized as follows: The child is extremely hyperactive, with a short attention span. He has many nervous mannerisms, such as incessant talking, picking at his nose until it bleeds, chewing holes in Tee-shirts and sheets, clearing his throat, and going through various physical contortions when he is very excited. Because of his hyperactivity, Harold is unable to keep his hands still for a moment, and he is very destructive of his toys, property in the home, and equipment at school. Harold seems jealous of other children and is very aggressive toward them. He is especially bossy and abusive toward younger children. However, he does not seem to realize that his behavior toward other children precipitates their retaliation and he feels that they pick on him unfairly. There have been instances when he has played with fire and his mother reports that when he was younger, he would kill birds and animals in a cruel manner. Harold craves attention and affection and is very trying on a foster parent's patience. When confronted with misdoings, his immediate impulse is to deny responsibility and blame other children. There was a time when Harold had become very preoccupied with playing war and seemed to be living in a fantasy world of "soldiers" with the Japanese as enemies. This had gone to the extent where he would sometimes get up in the night and dress in order to go out and stand guard duty.

Harold has just completed the third grade at school. He has attended approximately eight schools in his three years of school. He has had many teachers that have shown a special interest in him. This past year, he has been seen weekly by the social worker at school. Special attention from his teachers and the opportunity to meet with the social worker have helped Harold adjust to the school situation, but his functioning in that area is still inadequate.

summary

There is little possibility of finding a new foster home for Harold that will be able to put up with his present behavior, much less attempt to offer him the relationships he seems to need but does not accept. His father and stepmother are genuinely interested in him but will not keep him in their home until he can make a better adjustment. It is believed that residential treatment for Harold which will involve his father and stepmother offers the most hopeful future for this boy.

This chapter has presented some human service workers with varying degrees of training and from a variety of professional disciplines in their work with children. Some appeared to enjoy it more than others and some to have special talents that drew them to work with children. Obviously only a sample of the settings that involve children directly or indirectly could be included here. And even while this is being written it is probable that there are new kinds of services for children being planned and organized which will provide new and different approaches and opportunities for human service workers of all kinds.

questions

All the children discussed in this chapter were members of families. How did the human service workers described make use of what they knew of the relationships between the children and their families? How might they have done this?

Comment on the different ways in which the children and their families sent out signals and how they were received by the human service workers. How might they have been received by people in their every day lives who were not able to decode the messages?

It has been said that settings affect communication. Why did the 13-year-old pregnant girl confide in the white foster care aide on the subway when she refused to discuss her problem with the black woman counselors in the agency office?

This chapter has dealt with only a few settings where human service workers come in contact with children. Name some others.

additional reading

Charnley, Jean. *The Art of Child Placement.* Minneapolis: Univ. of Minnesota Press, 1955. Written for social workers doing foster care placement and supervision, this book provides many insights into the feelings of children, their foster parents, and own parents. Case studies, interestingly reported, describe work with babies, grade-school-age children, and adolescents. The questions that face foster care workers in planning for the most helpful kind of care—foster family, small group home, institution—give the reader the opportunity to participate in the decisions that will affect the course of the lives of many children.

Deloria, Vine, Jr. *Custer Died for Your Sins: An Indian Manifesto.* New York: Macmillan Co., 1969. Past executive director of the National Congress of American Indians, the author gives an authoritative, angry, and often ironically humorous account of Indian people in modern America, how they are regarded by white Americans, and what they want and need. The reader is left with a sense of the strength and endurance of Indians in the face of centuries of neglect and oppression. The human service worker will be able to translate some of what is said about Indians to increase his understanding of human nature types and fixed attitudes toward any minority group. Vine Deloria has also written *We Talk, You Listen, New Tribes, New Turf* (New York: Macmillan Co., 1971), an analysis of modern society with especial emphasis on the roles and strategy of modern movements for social change.

Ryan, William. *Blaming the Victim.* New York: Pantheon Books, 1971. The emphasis in *The Human Services* is placed largely upon individuals in interaction in the human services. Therefore it is essential for the reader to learn more about some of the social conditions which contribute to the problems of individuals. *Blaming the Victim* is an especially stimulating, though painful, account of social conditions and the kind of thinking of many well-intentioned people which perpetuates them. Whether or not the views expressed are over simplified, they have great impact and will be thought provoking for readers willing to make the effort to understand them.

Lukens, Kathleen and Carol Panter. *Thursday's Child Has Far to Go.* Englewood Cliffs, N. J.: Prentice-Hall, 1969. A brain-damaged little boy, a diabetic school girl, a child with Downs syndrome, and a baby with a crippling congenital disease are the central figures in the fictionalized accounts in this book. The responses of their families, friends, schools, doctors, and hospitals are all movingly described, giving the reader insights into feelings as well as behavior, in easy-to-read story form.

6 the human service worker and families

This chapter will present some families in need of help and some human service workers whose task was to help them. Of course, the children described in the last chapter might as easily have been placed in this one since each was a member of a family. The distinctions drawn between the chapters are based on the settings where people are met and on the emphasis of the service.

The family is the child's first environment. It is his world and how it receives him and what he learns there will influence what he will do in the world outside of his family and what he will expect in return. At the same time, the child influences the family. Profound family changes occur when a first child is born. Adjustments must be made for younger children. Other changes, positive and negative, come about from many causes. Much has been written about the adverse effects of divorce, alcoholism, parental unemployment or underemployment, and physical and mental illness. Changes occur, too, when "good" things happen to a family—a raise in salary that permits a move into a different social environment, perhaps with unfamiliar social customs, or the mother's going to work with its rise in income and perhaps a new center of interest for her. The outstanding scholastic or athletic skill or special talent of one member of a family may upset the equilibrium and life style of the whole family or of individuals in it.

In theory, most family counseling agencies and psychiatric clinics are available to all families in their communities who need some help in bringing their family life into a productive balance satisfying to all the members. But in actual fact public welfare services are the chief resource used by families whose difficulties are manifested by severe financial problems and inability to support themselves. For some, especially where there is a single parent or where the family consists of old people, little more than financial support may be needed. For many, however, both counseling and other human services such as homemaking, vocational training, and specialized medical care may be necessary. Human service workers having different levels of skill and training must often join forces to provide the help that is needed.

The great ideal of democracy—that all men are created free and equal and that all have equal opportunity to achieve what they want in life—may have a destructive effect when it gives rise to certain attitudes of the general public toward people who need the help of public welfare agencies. It sometimes seems as though the ideal is assumed to be the reality and that because individuals who need help are not achieving success, they are less worthy than those who maintain financial independence. If this kind of argument is used, it follows that a man who is a successful forger or a member of a well-organized crime syndicate is a better man than one who finds himself technologically unemployed and unable to support his family!

Probably few people actually believe that children in a home where inherited wealth makes for financial security are any better off than those where there is none—if both sets of parents are alcoholic, unfaithful to each other, and oblivious to the welfare of their children. Yet to be "on public welfare" is often seen as a sign of weakness, failure, and even willful laziness. What is more, human service workers in the public welfare field are sometimes seen as contributing to this sorry state of affairs or, at least, not changing it. This attitude has been an added burden for workers who were trying to help families struggling with many complex emotional relationships as well as with catastrophic "reality problems" which have no quick and easy solutions. For this reason, in the past there has been a high rate of turnover among human service workers in the public service agencies. Some of the best-trained workers came to prefer private agencies where they were not as tightly squeezed between the overwhelmingly difficult problems of their clientele and the unrealistic demands of taxpayers.

In recent years, however, there have begun to be interesting changes in both kinds of family services. Recognition of the contribution that human service workers with less than full professional training can make to agencies such as mental health services has motivated the employment of new kinds of staff. At the same time, the recruitment by public agencies of human service workers from the ranks of recipients has added to the interest and success of the work for professionally trained staff. In both kinds of settings, realization of the value of teamwork between human service workers from many different backgrounds and educational attainment is seen as a hopeful means of helping more people.

The following vignettes were chosen because they seemed to show how much interaction goes on within a family and between it and human service workers at every level of training. The excerpts are quite long and involved because family life is a long and complicated matter and the interactions within it do not lend themselves to quick and easy description.

When families lived near each other, it was assumed that if there was illness or misfortune in one household, the other relatives would take over its necessary tasks, indoor and outdoor, until they could be resumed. This kind of mutual help still goes on in many urban communities between friends or even, at times, acquaintances, but there are also many families whose relatives cannot give the help they need. Their problems may include severe illness or accident to the parents of young children, the increasing feebleness of old people, or the inability of parents to carry out the tasks needed for home maintenance although there are strong ties of affection. These families need help with home making—sometimes full-time help through a crisis, sometimes a few hours a week to take care of the chores an elderly couple cannot manage for itself. The alternative to such care—the separation of families and placement of members in foster care or institutions—is not only unhappy for the family but is extremely expensive for the community.

Some family counseling agencies, public and private, have added homemakers to their staffs to mitigate these situations. Most often, homemakers are women who have looked after their own families successfully, who have a demonstrated interest and concern for others, and who have the tolerance and maturity to work with people who may be difficult to get along with. The homemakers are usually not required to meet any particular educational requirements but are given some training in such areas as nutrition, first aid, and the general policy of the agency employing them. They are then assigned to cases, just as other staff members are. In most instances, they work closely with a caseworker or with a homemaker supervisor to whom they can turn for help or encouragement in their crucial but difficult daily contact with families in crisis.

family counseling service: homemaker

The homemaker quoted here talks about her work with one family in response to questions from the writer. She gives an eloquent account of what a person can accomplish using her own compassionate good sense and the support of professionals.

H: Where I was the homemaker last year she'd been married nineteen years, and then her husband left her for another woman, and she kind of had a stroke. She couldn't use her arm, her leg. She had to drag 'em. She couldn't speak. She was speechless. She'd maybe use one word, and then again she'd point.

INT: The husband had left her? She was all by herself?

H: Yes. No, she had two teen-age children, fourteen and thirteen. And the welfare was checking in on her and they didn't know if she was capable of continuing on as a mother and could keep a home together for these children, or if she ought to go to a nursing home and the children to foster homes. So they put me in the home to find out these things and perhaps help her. So I entered the home in October of last year. Our introductions were more or less a nod. I spoke, she just sat there and nodded.

INT: She knew you were coming?

H: Yes. The caseworker had asked her and she said she'd love to have someone come in. And her mother was there. Her mother put words in her mouth. She didn't let the lady try to think for herself. . . . Every time Helen'd look at me and say "coffee," her mother would look at me and say, "She can't talk. She means do you want a cup of coffee." I left it go the first time, the second time I said, "Ma'am, I'd rather Helen told me what she wants to tell me. She has to form those words." And then Helen would try to do things—

INT: Was she in bed, or—?

H: She was walking around but her hand was down and her arm was up and she was kind of pulling that one leg walking, just like a cripple when I went into the home and her eyes were sunk in her head and she looked really like a scarecrow. In fact, the caseworker thought, should we put her in the state hospital or what should we do with her? And this was—she said you should be in there a week or two to evaluate this and see what we should really do with her. And then when I went back and had a talk with the caseworker and told her that I'd like to work with the crippled lady if they wanted me to. She said, "Go ahead."

INT: But you really weren't sure, whether she was crazy or—?

H: I didn't think she was crazy because I knew she was nervous, and I knew she had problems bothering her. I knew her

From an unpublished interview. Used with permission.

mother upset her because every time her mother—even after that—would be there and her mother would do all the talking, she'd just sit there and she'd just pull her hands, her fingers, and finally I asked her if it was possible that Helen and I could just be alone when I was there. And her mother says, "Oh, all right." And the caseworker said that it would have to be that way because the mother was trying to get to move in with Helen so she could take care of her, and the caseworker said Helen would never get well, if the mother does. So we was trying to get through to Helen to get the mother out, because we was afraid the children would run away and Helen would get worse. And so it worked out. Grandmother didn't get moved in and Helen got better and the children are doing fine. . . . I don't know just exactly how we really got started communicating with one another, other than that I wouldn't answer her unless she spoke the word to me. If it took half an hour I would sit there and try to help her 'till she said the word herself.

INT: What gave you the idea of doing it this way?

H: It's the feeling you get when you walk into the home and you know what they need, when you see what they need. And like this woman is a shell and you want to see this woman revived. And it's a kind of a feeling you get when you work with people like this. You know they're good, you know they want to do things, and yet they're afraid. Because in her mind if she would start thinking, she would think about him again and she would put up a block. So over the period of weeks that I worked with her, every day little by little I began talking and asking different things about her husband. Maybe we would go through her pictures, his things, or mail would come for him, and I would talk about him. And I'd get her to talk about him. And beginning with the medical reports—day after day I spent with her at the Medical Center.

INT: Oh, you took her there?

H: Yes. I had a conference with the caseworker and her supervisor and I asked them if they thought that this was advisable, and they thought it was.

INT: Mmmm—what did they say at the Medical Center?

H: The Medical Center said that she had had a stroke and possibly there was some damage done to the brain, and this caused her arm to be numb, her speech, and her legs. And then they tested her and they couldn't find out why she wasn't beginning to function like she should. . . . We would play cards and

I would get her mind to thinking that way. We started out with aces and twos and threes together and then we started out mixing 'em up, and she responded to that. Then we started with dice and I'd make her count, and she started counting. And she was using her mind. She was getting her mind to actually function again. Through actually functioning with her mind I was teaching her how to cook by handfuls of flour, pinches of salt. She was making her own bread, doing her own cooking, and she even got so that we'd go to the grocery store and she could pick out the food and tell me all the labels, how much it weighed, how much the price of it was, and help me figure the budget, so she didn't spend more for her food than she was allowed. So by this she began functioning. I'd never permit her to make her bread with her good hand. It'd take us longer—it'd take us quite a while—but we had a marvelous time. And I was in her home every afternoon so that gave me quite a length of time. And she did all of her own cooking, but never with her good hand. And I told her I had a bad hand too, and we wouldn't use our good hands, we'd use our bad hands. So we both did this way. She functioned this way.

INT: Did you really have a bad hand?

H: No—(both laughing). I told her it didn't work right when I had to knead bread and I got her to knead bread, and she just enjoyed it. She makes beautiful bread now. She thinks for herself. She sews for herself. She cleans her house. She goes to the laundromat now and knows how to count her money. She cashes her check. She knows which envelope for each thing in the budget. And she's making it marvelous. She's just doing a great job. But there's a lot of things that needs to be said that haven't been said for her. It wasn't easy for her because she had to face reality. And this is the hardest thing in the world, to get a woman that's been rejected to face reality, because she knows that he has been running around and now knows he's living with another woman. But she made up her own mind and faced it enough now that she's suing for divorce, and she wants to meet a new friend and wants to remarry. I keep telling her every day, she's beautiful and she fixed her hair and she looked marvelous. Now she goes to the caseworker—she don't wait for the caseworker to come to the house—if she's got problems, she goes to the office. And they just admire her. She always looks so neat, so pretty. And she drives her own car now. And she's really alive now again.

INT: How old is she?

H: She's 39 years old. She's a beautiful woman.

INT: How long did you go in every afternoon?

H: I went in every afternoon since last—I think it was six months ago when I first started—and I stopped about a month ago, when school was out. But it wasn't all easy for either of us— like to teach her how to say a sentence. Like, I used to come there and she'd say, "coffee?" And I'd say, "Thank you, yes, thank you." And then one day I walked to the door and she'd practiced all morning long 'till I got there, and she said, "Mary— do—you—want—some—coffee?" And that was the biggest reward in Heaven for me, to hear her say that. I grabbed her and I cried and we cried. That to her—to give me that was so thrilling.

Then we had teen-age problems in the home, and the caseworker asked me if there was something I could do about it. The children liked me, they confided in me. And the one boy one Friday night late, oh about six o'clock I guess it was, he was with some boys, and they stole some beer out of the grocery store, was going to sell it to make money. I saw how Sam felt. They were on welfare and he didn't have no money, any money for anything and I knew how he felt and understood how he felt, but he told me. He didn't want to tell me at first because he was so ashamed because he didn't think I'd like him. But the letter came from the Juvenile Department for him to be in a meeting. He says, "Oh, please. . . ." The letter was laying on the table and when I came to that, I was opening the mail and reading her her mail and this was there. And he put his hand over the top of this, and he says, "Please, Mary, don't open that letter. I'll tell you about it first." So he told me about it. And I said, "Well, let's see what they got to say." Then it said that he had to be in court. So I said, "Well, we'll go to court." And we went to court and he held my hand, his daddy—I called his father and told his father I think it's time to stand by his son. And the mother, when we were in there talking to the Juvenile Officer, didn't pay any attention to the boy; she was looking up and down at her husband's shirt, see if he had any marks on him and things like this. She was really alert and I could see he was eyeing her, you know, and her little boy sitting there holding my hand. Wondering what's going to happen to me, you know, and they was wondering, gee, what happened to you, you know. And they was eyeing one another. But they dismissed it for Sam, "If you do what the Homemaker said and mind and not get into any more trouble." And Sam was so happy, we all were. The court counselor was very nice, permitting me—I'd called and asked if I could come.

Called and asked my caseworker and she said, "Certainly you can go." So I went to be with Sam. Then the father took the mother and Sam out for coffee. They invited me but I said I had a meeting at the welfare office, so I stepped out so they could go alone. But the father and mother I don't think will ever go back together again. And I prepared her for this. There's a possibility just because her love is still there, doesn't mean his—and I had to come right out and tell her. This woman had nothing to offer as a wife and mother or anything. She was gone. She has now, but she didn't. Six years she laid in this home like this.

INT: You mean this has been going on—you mean he had been going with another woman all that time?

H: For six years—she had been getting into this frame of mind for over six years, and then when he actually left her, she had this stroke.

INT: Well who looked after the kids all that time?

H: They just took care of themselves. And the caseworker says she don't think they ever had a hot meal, or anything like that. A can of soup or something. But they get it now. And she'd say, well Cathy—Cathy's home from school—"Cathy, get busy and cook supper." I said, "Helen, Cathy doesn't cook supper. Cathy's not the mother, you are, remember?" "Oh, yes, yeah, that's right, I forgot." And then every night when those kids come home from school she'd have some stew or something for 'em for supper. I said, "The kids can help with the dishes, but you're home all day and you can cook the supper and you're supposed to have it ready." She'd always sit there and say, "Oh, I forgot." And I'd say, "We forget things because we want to forget 'em." And she'd say, "That's right, that's right." So I got so I'd make a list of things for her to remember, and a list to do and don'ts. And she liked that.

INT: Do you think she was once smarter than she is now, or do you think she never was too, too—

H: No, no, because she wasn't taught how to keep house. She wasn't taught how to clean. She wasn't really taught how to take care of her children. And she don't know how to cope with the teen-age problems. She don't understand the situation of it. Her escape now is, "I have to go to a meeting at church, and something has to be done with those children." Well, the children are too old to be babysitted, and they will not go to church that they don't believe in and they don't like it, so I asked her then to get her mother or somebody to stay with the children.

And the children run the grandmother off. Grandmother can't get along with them—grandmother wouldn't permit 'em to have a friend over. Grandmother—nine o'clock you go to bed, and you do this and you do that, and only do what grandmother wants. And then I had to straighten the children out. Remember grandmother is here and grandmother is doing the best that she can do in her own way, and help grandmother instead of hurt grandmother. And Helen was in the hospital for about seven days and I was called at 11 o'clock at night, and by 2 o'clock in the morning I had the family all—Helen in the hospital, grandmother brought to town to stay with the children, and they fought and didn't want grandmother. And I had to put down the law. "All right, you don't want grandmother, we'll have to use Children's Protective Custody then. I'll have to call the police and have them take you or something. I have no one to call at this time in the morning and I'm doing the best that I can do. You *are* going to stay with grandmother and you *are* going to do what grandmother says, *aren't* you." They were marvelous the whole time grandmother was there. But I checked with them as if I was right in the house every afternoon, and I made my trips to the hospital every day to see Helen. . . .

The caseworker asked me to take a ride in her car with Helen—see how she drives and if you feel she's capable of driving. Otherwise we'll do something to stop her from driving that car. And I looked up to the heavens and I said, "Look, God, you know this is in the line of duty." So we got in the car and she went through the first stop sign, and I said, "Didn't you see that STOP back there?" She says, "Where? Oh, I haven't been stopping there." I says, "Well, start from now on." And after that driving down the road, she says, "Are you scared of my driving?" No—I'm cool, calm and collected, I was just smiling. Then I'd take her shopping to get her out of the house and to introduce her to the world and I'd say, "Go outside and look at the trees and say, 'Hello, tree, here I am. I'm Helen. Who are you?' " And I'd say, "Talk to anyone, just keep talking so the words will come back in your mind." And I'd take her to all—she'd drive that car and we'd go to the Goodwill and everywhere else. And she'd say, "How much is this?" And I'd say, "What does the price tag say?" And we'd stand there and we'd read them price tags on them things. Pretty soon she'd holler, "I found something for a quarter!" And she was learning the prices of things and how to say the words. . . . When I first started working with her I felt I had to get through to her that somebody cared, and for her to like herself. She felt so rejected and yet she was punishing herself because she had nothing to give.

The best thing that really happened for her was when he finally left home and lost his job and she *had* to have help from the welfare. Maybe if she had got it before and talked things over with a caseworker they wouldn't have broke up. She told me she objected to everything her husband did. He wasn't permitted—he liked to come home, sit down and watch TV and have a cold beer. She didn't permit that because she said her religion didn't permit it. Well, this man couldn't get it at home, he'd go somewhere else and get it. And she wouldn't go—she wasn't his wife. She didn't want—couldn't be bothered with him and—I got her to talk about all these things. And she says a lot of the troubles *were* her troubles, because she really didn't know how to act as a wife or a homemaker or a mother. They just existed and that was all.

INT: Did you talk about that a lot?

H: Yes. I got her to talk about it all the time. Now it's nothing for her to talk about it. She even told the lawyer all about it. Her husband asked her not to get the divorce. And yet he doesn't want to come back and live with her. She says, "What would you do?" And I says, "I don't know what I would do in your—you're going to have to decide." She's going to get the divorce, and I think she's glad to be strong enough to do it. Before, she was thinking of evil things to do to him. "I'd do this to him, I'd do that to him." I said, "Yes, but your light's not going to shine very bright if you do." I said, "You're a Christian woman, just think of that." I said, "Are you hiding behind this Christianity, or are you administering it where it's supposed to be? This isn't right for the children, to see you do evil things. How are you going to train them?" . . .

She's getting along fine now. When I have free time, I call her, or she has free time, she calls. And to see her smile—you wouldn't think it was the same person. I took her last month—I had an afternoon off and I always go get elderly people surplus foods for 'em when I get time off, and I go in and haul it for 'em and take it to their homes. And she was in there. My son and I helped her load her things. And she just run across that building, threw her arms around me and hollered, "Mary, Mary!" And she didn't stutter. She didn't keep still the whole time I was there. I knew everything that happened from the time I left the home 'till up to date. . . .

INT: Well, how do you work it that these kids who see what a mother can be like—you—how do you keep this going with their mother?

H: By having them understand their mother, that she has been ill, she would be this way if they help her. And she can't if she doesn't have help. And I says, "She'll do for you, if you'll do for her." And they do their work this way. Like on Friday nights, she likes to go to church. So the girl and the boy roam. So we made an agreement. Mama'll take them skating if they stay home and guard the house, so nobody'll break in. So they stay home and guard the house or they don't go skating. Then I work on her to take them skating (laughing) so that they can guard the house. So you know, you have to catch the children one way and her another, and tell her that the children don't know if she don't help teach 'em, and tell them that—you know—vice versa, to get 'em to work together. That's the way I do, but it worked out very nicely. They accepted it, that I was leaving. They knew that I was only there temporarily, and when it was time for me—they didn't like for me to go. At first they'd become dependent on me and it was up to me to break that dependency and put it on each other, which you can't do over night either. The kids didn't at first come right out and say, "Oh, boy, Mary, I sure like you." It had to be a work project. You had to get the kids to like you, to trust you. And then they begin to do the work and then they begin to do the dishes, dump the garbage, and cut the grass. It wasn't an easy project, but it had to be a long patient one. You had, as they say, to keep it cool. Many days I'd like to have just took both of 'em and, you know. . . .

So now the girl writes the letters for the mother that I always wrote, and the boy runs to the post office for the mother, where he didn't run before, and they do something for one another. . . .

So many little things went into it all. Like the first time she made her bed herself. We came back from the laundry and had clean sheets and things like that and she says, "Sam, you'll have to make the bed." And I says, "Sam, don't make the bed." She says, "Sam always has to make the bed." "No, Helen's going to make the bed." She says, "I can't." I said, "Oh, but Helen can." Then she went in there and she worked and she worked, but she got it. And then I says, "Isn't that pretty? Isn't that bed nice?" And she went and got Cathy and the neighbor lady and everybody else to come in and see that pretty bed that she made. But just little things like that. And the time she took the mop bucket and lifted the mop and the bucket, too. She says, "Look what I did!" And to her that was everything. To me that was a lot, too!

I was working with her to get her to please herself, to be happy within herself. Then she would have happiness around her.

INT: How did you get these kinds of ideas yourself? You haven't been a Homemaker all that long—

H: No, I had worked in community work for over three years. I'd always had—was always helping neighbors. I've always done it, and I always will continue 'cause I feel this is my life work. If I go on to something else, other than a Homemaker, I'll always be a community worker. . . . I came from a large family. Each one helped each other. And we grew up like this. My mother always told us that when we didn't love ourself, we didn't love anyone. And I had embedded this in my children's minds, and I hope that it's the right philosophy.

INT: Where did she get that from?

H: My mother? I imagine from her mother. My mother was full-blooded Cherokee Indian. And she was a wonderful woman. I had a wonderful father. So I have—if you have love to give, why not? You know, it's not invented. It's something within yourself. I've never—well my kids come home and say love, peace, you know, and I say, "Where did you hear the word love before?" "Oh, we heard that growing up." So, this isn't new.

You have to have compassion for people and want to let them know you care. Majority of people we work for have been beat down so far in the world that when they get a lift up and then they're knocked down so many times, they become—anyone comes in their home it's just—they're distrustful about 'em. You *have* to let them know that you yourself care about 'em. Then knowing that you care for them and what they do, they try real hard. They try, real, real hard. And they're marvelous people, great.

INT: Depends on who—

H: Well—that's true, but regardless—I don't know, the worst—somewhere there's—lift up something—you have to find it. Just to be able to stand up after you've been knocked down fifty times, you have to have something. But some people *are* awful hard. I asked my caseworker yesterday in a meeting to get me off of this case I'm on now and she says, "oh, OK." And when we talked about it and when the meeting was over, she said, "Do you really want off this?" I said, "Forget it."

INT: (Laughing) Why did you want to get off it?

H: Off the case? (sigh) It's a referred case from the court—question of divorce or custody or placement—and it's three children involved and my purpose in the home is for child care, cooking, and see that the mother does her housework. It's everything opposite—him and her's fighting all the time. So it's not all pleasant.

INT: No, you bet it isn't.

H: To get 'em to stop one day I had to say, "I don't stay in homes that bicker like this. I've got to leave. I don't care to stay in here. I'm going back to the office." He says, "I'll stop and you stay." So I'm still there!

Helen and her family profited from the partnerships between the homemaker, professional social workers, and the doctors. The homemaker could report to the professionals many small first-hand observations on which they could base decisions and suggestions to guide the homemaker's next steps.

The homemaker is so articulate and explains her reasons for her actions so clearly that there is little need for additional comment on her remarkable achievements with a situation which looked quite hopeless at the beginning. It may be worth noting, however, that the homemaker, understanding the part a public welfare case-worker might have played if she had been in contact with the family early in their difficulties, regrets that they did not have to make use of public welfare sooner. She recognizes that most people see an application for public welfare as a last resort and perhaps as a degrading admission of failure, while she sees it is an opportunity to get much needed help with many problems, not only financial ones.

It is plain throughout this account that the homemaker was one of those talented people who somehow see and hear more of the invisible and unspoken than most people do. She is able to understand and accept the behavior and the feelings of other people as well as her own. This allowed her to make a large investment of time, energy, and love in Helen and her family and, at the same time, to strengthen the bonds between them so that they no longer needed her and she could turn her talents to helping other families. Terminating an arrangement in which so much has been invested is never easy. The homemaker describes a most thoughtful and successful resolution of a situation which arises in almost every human service contact.

graduate school
of social work:
the browns

Professional social workers (those holding the MSW degree) have had two years of graduate education which has included theories of personality and social development and a study of social problems and methods of helping individuals and groups. They have had a supervised field work experience designed to integrate theory and practice. The report quoted below was written as a class assignment in casework by a second year student in a school of social work. The assignment was to present a case known to her in her field work placement and lead class discussion of it as the student might expect to do in the future as a case supervisor or teacher.

the brown family

Roger Brown, 28; Martha Brown, 23; Michael, 6; Donald, 3; Tom, 2; Peter, 6 months.

Although the Brown family has been known periodically to various service agencies including Public Welfare, my contact with the family has been through the University Medical School Social Service Department. All of my referrals have come from the Pediatric Clinic. Social services are usually of short duration, such as arranging for nursing home placement, planning transportation for patients, or doing social history and evaluation for a psychiatric referral. Most work is done at the clinic, but as a student I have been able to make home visits and provide continued casework services in some instances.

Mrs. Brown was referred to me because of marital difficulties which were intensified by the birth of a son, Peter, with cystic fibrosis. Basically, cystic fibrosis is a congenital disease characterized by the formation of heavy mucous in the lungs, preventing proper functioning. There is as yet no cure though life can sometimes be prolonged through childhood. The disease is treated by physical therapy which drains the lungs. Peter's treatments had to be administered three or four times daily. The referring doctor was concerned about Mrs. Brown's ability to

From an unpublished case study. Used with permission.

continue adequate care for Peter on discharge from the hospital. There was concern because Mr. Brown did not appear to assist his wife or be supportive and the doctor felt that Mrs. Brown's emotional state was poor and that complete dysfunction seemed probable.

My first contact was with Mrs. Brown when she brought Peter in for a check-up. She is tall and slender, and looked physically and emotionally exhausted. She has an attractive face, but her eyes were listless. She chain smoked and told me in a monotone that "Life was a bore," and that she "didn't give a damn anymore." During this interview and the ones that followed, I have gained a story of a life torn by poverty and lack of emotional nourishment.

Mrs. Brown remembers none of her life prior to the age of ten. Her mother spent little time with the children. She always worked and sometimes stayed away for days at a time. One year she was a professional prostitute and boarded the children out. According to Mrs. Brown, her mother was a beautiful woman who always wore beautiful clothes. The children were clothed in second-hand clothes and hand-me-downs. Mrs. Brown was the second of four children. Mother married a series of men, all nonworkers who drank to excess. Mrs. Brown was molested by the first of her three step-fathers from the age of ten until twelve. She thought her menstrual cycle was the result. Her mother divorced the step-father, but pressed no charges. Later, Mrs. Brown's mother accused her of "leading him on." Mrs. Brown told me this in a matter-of-fact tone, but added with a short laugh, "as if any twelve-year-old could do that." Mrs. Brown was finally removed from her mother's home and placed in a foster home. Mrs. Brown maintains that the foster home straightened her out in terms of preventing her from becoming a "tramp." In the foster home, Mrs. Brown was given guidance and firm limits. She thinks highly of her foster parents and they still visit and maintain contact. Mrs. Brown says it is like Christmas when they visit because they give the family so much. While in the foster home, Mrs. Brown did well in school. A year later, she was returned home and was disappointed to find that the home had not changed as she had been dreaming it had.

At the age of fifteen, Mrs. Brown met Roger Brown, five years her senior. He was a "quiet, shy boy." They wanted to marry, but her mother forbade this. Martha dated only this boy, but her mother accused her of running around with everyone. When Martha became pregnant, consent for marriage was given.

Mr. Brown began beating his young wife on the wedding night and physical abuse has continued. During pregnancy, Mr. Brown thought his wife "ugly, big and not pretty anymore." He was not a comfort during the pregnancy; neither was her mother. Mrs. Brown resents Mike even now because she "took beatings for him."

Mr. Brown is a slight man of twenty-eight whose hands shake visibly, perhaps as a result of heavy drinking. He is partially deaf, talks loudly and gives the impression of being cocky. Mr. Brown was hospitalized from the age of eight months until age four, though no diagnosis is available. He was then raised by his mother and step-father. The step-father had a poor work record, drank heavily and fought constantly with his wife. The step-father to this day tells Mr. Brown that he is "no good, a bum, and a person who will never amount to anything." Mr. Brown has never held a job for more than eight months, though he is a boiler maker who can earn $300.00 to $600.00 a month. He complains of frequent illness, such as asthma, and simply doesn't go to work and is then fired. When he gets drunk he beats up his wife. He doesn't hit the children since Mrs. Brown "hit him over the head with a skillet."

The same year Mike was born, Mrs. Brown lost a baby. A year later, she lost another. In 1963, a son, Don, was born. A year later, Tom was born. The following summer Mrs. Brown had a severe case of hepatitis and almost died. She went directly from the hospital to assume her home responsibilities. Mr. Brown was interested in another woman and declared, "I wish you *had* died, you son-of-a-bitch." A month later, Mrs. Brown was pregnant with Peter and he was born with cystic fibrosis. The exhaustion from the hepatitis and marital discord were intensified by the care Peter required.

diagnosis and treatment

I formed the diagnosis of an emotionally neglected couple, unable to give each other much support or love because they had not received any. The emotional development of both Mr. and Mrs. Brown was retarded by deprivation, neglect and loss. Thinking of this on a continuum, Mr. Brown seems less developed than Mrs. Brown and functions on an infantile level. Treatment had more chance of success with her though there were great obstacles to a hopeful outcome.

The diagnosis of emotional deprivation meant the treatment

would be to provide a relationship which would encourage ego growth. Mrs. Brown cannot learn to give unless she is given to. Supportive techniques were used to strengthen Mrs. Brown and achieve the goal of better care for Peter. Weekly visits were decided upon.

There are industrial railroad tracks at the end of the block and a trucking company is located around the corner of the Brown's home. There is no yard to speak of, as the house is up on a bank. The oldest boy, Mike, is failing the first grade and was threatened with suspension. The three- and two-year-olds cannot talk and they always have two fingers in their mouths.

The weekly visits also revealed that Mrs. Brown has artistic talent, enjoys drawing, flower arranging, and changing room arrangements. I encouraged Mrs. Brown in her drawing, as I felt it was important for the development of identity. Mrs. Brown also builds things out of practically nothing—beds out of old doors and large jars, a coffee table out of wood scraps and a piece of glass, a knickknack shelf out of a wooden box, for instance. The art work has turned out to be an important means of expression for Mrs. Brown.

The casework situation became even more difficult when, in December, Mrs. Brown would not be home or at least didn't answer the door during the regular home visit time. In January, her husband, who had broken his ankle, was in the clinic and I talked to Mrs. Brown about her avoidance of me. I learned that her husband had made so many comments about her "getting her head straightened and go talk to your social worker," that she had thought it easier not to see me. She explained that Mr. Brown became upset when anyone paid her much attention. When Mr. Brown returned from x-ray, I talked to him about his foot, made some comments, and again reviewed my purpose in seeing the family as one of helping with Peter. I hoped this would take some of the pressure off of Mrs. Brown.

As all families need vacations from intensive care members, I suggested a short period at the Babies' Clinic for Peter, which would be paid for by the Division. The family was interested in a short vacation. Cystic children gain weight slowly, but Peter was doing less well than most—at the age of six months he weighed only eight pounds. According to Mrs. Brown, both she and her husband were "afraid of babies." She had told me before that she couldn't help feeling that Peter's slow weight gain reflected lack of care on her part. She had also told me that she had had a dream in which Peter was suffocating under blankets, and the more she tried to pull them away from his face the more blankets appeared—he died and *she did it*. She hadn't told anyone else this because it "didn't seem important." I told her it was obvious that she was concerned about Peter.

Three days after the cited interview, Peter Brown died. My efforts to locate temporary care for Peter had failed. The guilt feelings I experienced were minor compared to those suffered by Mrs. Brown, whose husband accused, "You *let* him die!" The main techniques used to support Mrs. Brown were acceptance, help with the funeral arrangements, and ventilation. In the latter I listened and accepted Mrs. Brown's feelings about Peter's death. Reassurance was given regarding her efforts to do the best for Peter. She was reminded that she had assumed all responsibility for Peter, was not in good health to begin with, had the flu, but had always done the best she could. As she wanted all physical reminders of Peter removed, I transported medication back to the clinic. She thanked me again and again and we made a home visit appointment for the following week. The children and Mrs. Brown seemed more relaxed after Peter's death.

After Peter's death, Mrs. Brown announced to me that from then on she was going to handle the money in the family. It is interesting to note that Mr. Brown thought this was a good idea, in contrast to her expectation when I had suggested the plan to her months ago. Financial problems have always existed in this family, and they went through bankruptcy in the first year of their marriage. Mrs. Brown had always carried the money in her purse, did not handle it, but gave it to her husband knowing full well that he would drink it up. So, on the immediate level her action meant she was willing to take responsibility for a problem, and that her ambivalence was overcome. Naturally there have been regressions at times of greater stress. This step by Mrs. Brown suggests ego incorporation of a problem-solving process. She had a focus area for the immense marital problems in the family.

Mrs. Brown indicated a desire for help in the area of marital problems, so this is now the identified problem. Ideally, of course, both partners would be seen, but this is impossible. So I have concentrated on emotional nourishment for Mrs. Brown, who really is the nourishment source for the whole family. The diagnosis is of an emotionally deprived married couple living together, but remaining apart emotionally. Communication is mainly in the form of physical blows.

In working with this family I have learned that, in a manner typical of emotionally deprived people, they communicate through actions not words. For example, Mrs. Brown indicated her feelings about my visits, not through words, but through behavior avoidance. Mr. Brown communicates his feelings about his unhappiness with himself through his excessive drinking. Later in my work with the family, Mrs. Brown told me she liked me by drawing a picture for me. This form of communication did not change my diagnosis or treatment goal, but it certainly has affected my methods. Verbalizing as a treatment technique probably has not been as important as my actions.

Mrs. Brown began describing constant headaches and the need for something for her "nerves." It has been noted that people who suffer emotional neglect or deprivation express their inner hurt by means of physical ailments, frequently severe headaches and insomnia. These seem to be more intense when the client is attempting some change in his life pattern. I made an appointment for Mrs. Brown, took her to the clinic, and baby-sat the children while she was seen. Behavior, as previously discussed, was the communication system used to show Mrs. Brown that I will help. (Mr. Brown soon began taking Mrs. Brown's nerve pills to get to sleep.)

Several weeks ago I asked Mrs. Brown about attending an art class at the Community Center, where babysitting would be provided. I urged her on the basis of a need for some time of her own, and enriching her art talent. She didn't act very interested, but two weeks ago she casually mentioned going to the evening class (requiring a babysitter as Mr. Brown won't stay with the children), with her friend, Andrea. The class is doing mosaics and she expressed surprise, and by the look on her face, pleasure, that people were envious and praising of her ability to make her own pattern. The teacher asked to keep the pattern. She told me all her family members had art talent and she thought everyone did. I encouraged her to see this talent as a unique quality she possesses. I do not expect great movement in this case as far as marital change, but I think Mrs. Brown is moving toward an image of herself as an individual with her own identity.

home visit, march 13

Don and Tom were put to bed for a nap. The living room was filled with washing and we sat in the middle of it on the sofa. As she proceeded to sort and fold clothes, Mrs. Brown told me that her husband had surprised her by taking the laundry and drying it Sunday evening. She said she hadn't had time to sort the clothes earlier, because she had been doing hair-dos and make-up jobs for people in the neighborhood and generally received $1.50 or babysitting in exchange for this.

I asked how the week-end had gone and Mrs. Brown told me that on Saturday her husband had really surprised her by taking her to a drive-in movie. They had gone by themselves, sat in the back row and "necked." Mrs. Brown expressed the belief sarcastically that she thought probably the snow on Monday was the result of her husband doing such a surprising thing. We both laughed.

I told Mrs. Brown that in thinking over Mike's situation at school (threatened suspension) I had become quite concerned about the problem he was having. I expressed the belief that Mike would not be able to pass the first grade and Mrs. Brown concurred with this. She said that he already was going to half a day of kindergarten and half a day of first grade. The problem at school had been Mike's reluctance to mind the teacher. I suggested that the difficulty she and her husband were having might be affecting Mike and his ability to pay attention at school. She recalled how her own home situation had made it impossible to function at school, but then she dropped the cause-effect recognition. Mrs. Brown did not feel that any action on her part in connection with the school was warranted. She has seemed reluctant, in my contacts with her, to exert herself for Mike.

I also returned to the former week's interview when I told Mrs. Brown I wondered what she had meant when she said her husband felt she was "over-interested" in the kids. Mrs. Brown, who appears outwardly passive, surprised me by blurting out in an angry tone, "That's just it, he wants all the attention."

She went on to tell me that lately she had not been taking as much guff from her husband. I had urged her to tell him things such as how she felt, etc. Although I didn't think what she said would have too great an effect on Mr. Brown, I thought it important that she express herself rather than hold everything in and then exploding by hitting her husband. I asked Mrs. Brown if telling her husband what she thought made her feel any better, and she said that well, she didn't feel any better.

As it seemed important at this time to discover just what Mrs. Brown's interest in change in the family was, I asked her what she would like to change in the marriage, if there were things she felt could be changed. Her main concern was with Mr. Brown and his drinking. She said that was the one thing she would like to change in the marriage. She vehemently stated that she was not going to change anymore. I asked her what she meant and she talked about the change she had made in relations. She defined relations as sex relations and her frigidity. She said that for the first three years of her marriage to Mr. Brown she wouldn't even undress in front of him. She also stated that she had settled down and that both of them had run around at the beginning of the marriage but that she did not do this anymore. Mrs. Brown went on to say that she had become a better housekeeper and cook. She went back to the old phrase about not caring any more. I felt that Mrs. Brown's actions expressed just the opposite and I said that although she had told me this, she made every effort to keep the family going, by cooking their meals, cleaning the house and all the other chores she performs. Mrs. Brown does exhibit a strength in meeting the physical needs of her family.

Mrs. Brown, as noted earlier, has artistic talent and likes to try experimenting with flower arrangements and other things around the house. She doesn't have much of an opportunity to get out of the house. In order to "mother" Mrs. Brown, I asked her if she would like to go to the Import Bazaar with me in two weeks and she smiled, looked very pleased, and said yes. I told her we could take the children, but that I didn't know whether they would be interested. She expressed the belief that it would be too difficult for them not to touch things and that she would get a babysitter. She talked about saving a dollar or so out of her husband's check so that she could buy something. When I left, making a date for two weeks from the 13th, Mrs. Brown thanked me for coming out and said she would see me soon.

questions

These questions are representative of those I would use in discussing the case with a supervisor or casework student.—A.C.

1. Readings often refer to starting with the client "where he is." Based on your knowledge of ego development, where would you place Mrs. Brown? Mr. Brown? Support your view by passages in the case material.

2. On the basis of your development evaluation, do you think one parent has more potential for ego growth?

3. What defenses do you think Mrs. Brown exhibits? Support your answer with passages from the material.

4. Can you pinpoint one major problem that offers a key point of attack in helping the family?

5. In the case background material and interview, can you find examples of teaching?

6. What evidence do you find that the deprivation pattern is repeating itself?

7. What suggestions, questions, or criticisms do you have concerning the family, case record, or worker activity?

8. What significance might this type of family have in terms of American social problems and future welfare programs?

The major difference between the graduate student's approach and that of the homemaker is that the student based her work on principles of personality theory about development, which she had learned from her studies, while the homemaker relied only on her own intuition and personal experience. The student made an estimate of the potential of the Browns for change and a deliberate and conscious choice of method to bring this change about. By doing so, she could check on her own progress and verify her original impression or revise it in accordance with her experience. She made consistent use of one of the several theories of personality development which she had studied in graduate school to guide her actions in this very difficult and tragic situation. She knew, therefore, that change would come slowly, if at all, and that her own role must be one of patiently giving support and practical help if a relationship of trust were to be developed. She was well aware that little could be accomplished until Mrs. Brown, who had had few opportunities to learn to trust anyone, could let the worker help her carry her appalling load of real problems.

Though the worker does not indicate in detail how she learned about Mrs. Brown's unhappy past, it is safe to assume that she did so little by little, over a period of time and in answer to questions carefully adjusted to Mrs. Brown's difficult situation and her first statements. One may assume, too, that when the worker heard the words "life is a bore" spoken by Mrs. Brown, she also heard words that were not spoken—such as, "I can't manage alone; no one helps me with this overwhelming situation I am unprepared to carry," and "no one wants to help me." As she came to know Mrs. Brown better, the worker could speak words showing she did understand and would try to help; but more important, she could give Mrs. Brown the support that comes from knowing that someone heard her voice, that she was not alone.

Human service work with the mentally retarded illustrates how increase in knowledge affects the human services. One hundred years ago, the mentally retarded were not distinguished from the mentally ill. They were hidden in homes of relatives who were ashamed and afraid of them. Or they were placed in large congregate institutions which, though poor in our view, were a great improvement over the prisons or poorhouses to which many had been consigned in earlier times.

The differences in degree of retardation, the possibilities of training for some, the importance of achievement within the limits of one's handicaps came to be recognized by administrators of large institutions. As the families of mentally retarded people became better known to human service workers, views of mental retardation changed so that it was no longer seen as a sign of degeneracy or divine punishment for evil doing.

Some of the causes for mental retardation have been identified and some steps taken toward its prevention, although there is still much more to be learned. Today, most human service workers urge parents to care for their mentally retarded children at home and to give them as many of the experiences of normal children as possible, because it is believed that in this way the mentally retarded can live much more satisfying and useful lives than they can within the walls of institutions.

One consequence of this change in attitude is that human service workers at all levels and in many fields now come in contact with the mentally retarded. They may be met in schools, hospitals, nursing homes, and other institutions as patients or as members of the housekeeping staff. They participate in swimming classes, go to summer camps, work in sheltered workshops. Their families too, may be seen by doctors, psychologists, and social workers since there is no doubt that mental retardation in one member of a family subjects other members of the family to stresses that are at times almost intolerable.

Children may be retarded in intellectual development as the result of genetic defects which are just beginning to be understood, by injury at birth, or by accidents or illness in infancy and early childhood. Some retarded children have a minimal capacity for independent existence, while others can become quite independent, well-adjusted members of society. One group that is frequently seen by human service workers is sometimes referred to as mongoloid although the proper scientific name for their kind of retardation is Down's Syndrome. These children have certain physical characteristics in common. It is their rather flat, somewhat Oriental facial features which have led to the "mongoloid" designation. These children are usually considered to be "teachable," although some are hardly able to master intelligible speech, while others can learn to read and write on the level of a child in the primary grades.

retarded child
at home:
vicky

The following description of a child with Down's Syndrome from a prominent family makes note of many of the problems that confront the families of all retarded children. Their unusual ability to discuss their feelings about the child can help human service workers to appreciate both the difficulties and the attractive qualities of such children.

Vicky can write her name, and the names of her three younger sisters: Jill, Amy, and Cindy. She can tie a bow and likes doing it so well that, if she has a string of licorice, she would rather tie than eat it. She can be trusted to lift Cindy, who is two and and a half, out of her crib in the room that they share, and carry her downstairs to Mommy. When she gets her turn on the trampoline, she counts as she jumps, "One! Two! Three-four-five!" In school she is learning about hundreds, and this fall she graduated from her preprimer to a real reader. She rides a two-wheeler with training wheels, and a horse, and, in the words of her grandmother, she "swims like a little porpoise." At eleven years old, Vicky is a remarkable child; because she is mongoloid, every accomplishment, except her ready, trusting smile, has been very hard to come by. . . .

When Mrs. Humphrey talks of her granddaughter's problems and achievements, it is always against a backdrop of other children like Vicky. She is haunted by the little mongoloid children she saw on one of her many visits to a state institution. "They had nothing to do but sit on the floor and watch television," she says. "They didn't even know how to wave goodbye. They are all potential Vickys in my mind." Ever present in her mind, too, is the fact that Vicky came within a hairbreadth of being one of them. . . .

Everyone in the family remembers the night Vicky was born. Election night, 1960, was a time of incomparable joy. Shortly after the polls closed, it was clear that Hubert Humphrey had been reelected to the Senate. . . .

Excerpts from "A Special Child Indeed" by Vivian Cadden, McCalls, January, 1972. Reprinted courtesy of the author.

The Humphreys' first grandchild was born about 1:30 A.M. Mrs. Humphrey can recall no happier night in her entire life.

The baby was a hefty one: seven pounds, eleven ounces. Mrs. Humphrey and Bruce had a glimpse of her right after she was born. "She looked real cute," Bruce says. . . .

[Next day]

In the reception room on Nancy's floor the exuberant grandmother and father, he loaded down with cigars, were met by Nancy's obstetrician, who said to them, "What do you know about mongolism?"

"Odd terrors ran through my head," Mrs. Humphrey says— and eleven years later she is still close to tears as she recalls it. "I had these vague remembrances of a college psychology textbook. *Mongolism*. Just a word. I couldn't grasp the full meaning of what he was asking. I think I said, 'What do you mean? Is there something wrong with the baby?' And he said, 'We're not sure.' "

Knowing what she knows now about mongolism, Mrs. Humphrey believes that he must have been sure. He was simply unable to tell her outright. Mrs. Humphrey feels that he should have been candid with her, but with characteristic charity she says, "It isn't easy, no matter how you're told. Between the unparalleled joy of the night before—and now, this—it was probably the biggest drop that one could experience in life."

Sitting outside Nancy's door, numbly agreeing to a late-afternoon conference to verify the suspicions, Bruce and Mrs. Humphrey signaled without words their inability to talk to Nancy about this now. "Bruce is like a son to me," Mrs. Humphrey says. "But as close as we were, we had very little to say to each other."

They went in to see Nancy, and made cheerful noises, and fled. Mrs. Humphrey doesn't remember telling her husband about it that morning. She can't imagine how she summoned the courage to tell him ever. She still had no idea of the scope of what was facing them all. It was only a word: mongolism.

For all their caution—or probably, more precisely, because of it—Nancy knew. Something was amiss.

She had awakened that morning to see a doctor at the foot of her bed, and she had asked, "Is there something wrong?" He said, "How did you know?" Then he equivocated: maybe there was, maybe there wasn't. He asked her the same question, "What do you know about mongolism?" She didn't answer. "It didn't sink in," she says. "It didn't jell. I didn't know what he was talking about. I just wanted to be alone to think."

And so she and her husband and her mother kept their secret from one another that morning. No one was ready to believe it.

At 5:30 that afternoon, there was a conference at the hospital: Hubert and Muriel Humphrey, Bruce, their pediatrician, and a pediatric specialist from the University of Minnesota Medical School. There was no doubt that the baby was mongoloid. Her eyes, some of her reflexes, the straight line across the palm of her hand, all confirmed the diagnosis. Such a child needs to be institutionalized, the specialists said, and the suggestion was that this be done immediately.

Only the pediatrician was a little less dogmatic. . . . She might, he said, progress quite normally for a few months until the difference in her development became noticeable. His was the only intimation that the situation was anything but hopeless. . . .

The conference adjourned in unspoken agreement. Vicky— she didn't have a name yet—was to be institutionalized; but since the paths to that procedure were undiscussed and uncertain, the next steps were in abeyance. Ordinarily, such children were placed in foster homes until they reached the age of two or three, at which point they were put in a state institution.

Bruce went in to talk to Nancy alone, but they were not really able to talk. For Nancy it was still unreal. They had brought in the baby, and she had looked as a baby should. But the nurses were saying, "You don't take these babies home," or, "It's better if you don't get attached to them," or, "They're mean children, mongoloids."

"It was unbelievable," Nancy recalls.

Bruce left her then, to break the news to his parents. His mother says simply, "It was the darkest hour of my life." Vicky was her first grandchild, too.

Bruce remembers going home alone and looking at the room they had prepared for the baby. It had been freshly painted, and there was the crib that had belonged to Nancy's youngest brother. "I looked at that room," Bruce says, "and I said, 'To hell with it. I'm going to bring that baby home.' "

His mother-in-law was having similar thoughts. "I said to myself, this child has four grandparents, two parents, a room that is waiting for her at home," Mrs. Humphrey says. "How can there possibly be a better place for her than home? What foster parents, what institution can do more for her? Right then and there I decided that if Nancy and Bruce felt that they could not raise Vicky, I would." . . .

Senator and Mrs. Humphrey were careful not to give Nancy and Bruce any advice or to advocate any particular course, not that they really were sure themselves of what was right. What they did do was make available to the grieving young couple some expert counseling—not particularly to help them make a decision whether or not to keep Vicky . . . but to help them deal with their feelings about her, the sorrow and guilt and shame.

All the participants in the tragedy were struggling with these feelings. Whose fault was it? Was the bad seed a Humphrey or a Solomonson one? Nancy says, "You start off saying, 'Why us?' and 'What have I done to deserve this? Why did God do this to me?' And then you find yourself saying, 'But it can't be my fault. It must be from *his* family.' "

Fortunately, Nancy and Bruce did not pursue this line of thinking for long, and they were lucky in not having it dwelled upon by their parents. . . .

"The counseling was very important to us," Nancy says. "Every hospital ought to have it available on the spot for new parents who have to face such a problem." The Hennepin County social worker, the specialists from the University of Minnesota, and some professional friends of the Humphreys outlined the prospects for the baby, tried to give aid and comfort to her parents. . . .

When the baby was five days old, she was baptized. "I didn't want to give her a name that I really like," Nancy says, "so I named her Victoria, because of election night. It was a kind of impersonal name to me."

She was fighting to detach herself from this baby. "I'd lie there and think, 'She isn't really mine. It's just a baby I had. Someone else's.' I made her ugly in my mind, so as not to want her."

. . . Nancy's first concern was to get out of the hospital. The other babies on the floor "drove me crazy," she remembers. When Vicky was a week old, Nancy and Bruce took her home for what was to be a temporary stay until they could sort out the legal complications involved in making her a ward of the state.

. . . They went to visit a foster home. Nancy found it very depressing but tried not to think about it. "There were five or six little babies in cribs," Bruce says, "and it wasn't anything like a family. It appalled us."

At home, Vicky was a good baby and not particularly difficult to care for. Unlike some mongoloids at birth, she had only a slight heart murmur and few respiratory problems, and she had no trouble learning to suck. . . .

Once the shock and initial grief had worn off, Nancy and

Bruce simply felt that they wanted her, and that they were strong enough to raise her. Nancy recalls, "My pediatrician told me, 'Don't forget, that child is yours.' I realized she *is* my child, and we must do what's best for her."

Muriel Humphrey, now armed with expert knowledge and years of service on the President's Committee on Mental Retardation, does not feel that every family can manage a severely retarded child, or should. What she does feel, with great passion, is that no couple should make the decision about keeping or institutionalizing such a child in those first traumatic days. If there is one thing she asks of doctors, it is that they do not push mothers and fathers into a decision. No one needs to decide in the hospital, she says. No one should. The shock is so great, the fright and guilt and shame so overwhelming, that it is impossible to think. One needs to wait. Parents and grandparents alike.

Nancy thinks their decision to keep Vicky had something to do with the resilience of youth. She doesn't know whether now, at age thirty-two, with three other children in the family, she would keep a child like Vicky. "But I was twenty-one, and Bruce was nineteen, and life was beautiful. When you're young, things move on so fast that you can't stay grieving very long. The decision-making got us down, but once that was over, I don't remember moping or crying. Bruce and I take it better than my parents do. When you're older, things get to you more."

Very soon after they decided to keep Vicky, Bruce and Nancy had a series of genetic tests, and the doctors advised them to have another baby right away. Jill Solomonson will be ten in March. Amy will be seven, and Cindy is now two and a half. . . . All three of the other children are perfectly normal.

Meanwhile, there was Vicky, and a cruel little deceiver she was during her first year; for until a child begins to walk, run, and speak, and until hand-eye coordination and abstract thinking begin to emerge, the retarded infant may not seem so different or backward. This accounts for the fact that although mongolism is instantly recognizable to doctors, many other retarded and brain-damaged children go unrecognized as such during the first six months of their lives. Vicky's relative normality fed the fantasies of her family—who, although they had accepted her, were still loath to accept the extent of her limitations. . . .

"All during that first year we said, 'She's not so *much* different.' " . . .

When Vicky was two, Nancy started to look for a school for

her. Jill had been born by then, and Nancy and Bruce were beginning to seek some proportion in their lives. They knew that
Vicky could not dominate their whole existence—that they must
find some way to deal with her special problems, at the same
time allowing themselves and Jill a way of living and breathing
that would not be stifled by the demands of Vicky's affliction. . . .

If you ask Vicky what she does in school, she says quickly,
running the words together, "Work, puzzles, coloring books,
paper, crayon." This is a pretty good description of the Montessori method with its graded materials, its structure of "puzzles" that must be mastered one by one in a specific order, its
sense of "work" which must be started and continued and finished and put back exactly where it came from and as it came,
its use of cutting, pasting, and sorting, its emphasis on color
identification—all a prelude to and a foundation for the actual
learning of reading, and writing, and arithmetic. . . .

In one regard, however, Fraser School and Montessori are
very different. Montessori relies on self-discipline on the part of
children and goes to great pains to develop this. Fraser School
believes that a key factor in the handling of retarded children is
loving, yet very, very firm discipline.

Parents, Bob Kowalczyk finds, are all too often afraid to discipline a retarded child. The school must not be. The teacher, he
feels, "must put her foot down the very first day, and make it
clear that 'no' does not mean 'maybe.' She can't approach her
pupils with an attitude of 'you poor thing.' " Parents shouldn't
either, but that's hard to get across to them, Kowalczyk says. . . .

"We try to raise their expectations for their children, to show
them that in many ways they are more normal than abnormal,
to get parents to see that the child has skills, to rid them of
shame and guilt. It isn't easy." . . .

How far will Vicky go? No one knows for sure. The minimum
goals for a child who has advanced as far in school as Vicky has
are that she will "have the potential of obtaining some degree of
independence and self-care upon reaching adulthood." . . . And
when Vicky is ready for it, perhaps at twenty, there will be some
kind of vocational training to fit her for a job, whether out in the
big, frightening world, or in some kind of sheltered workshop
for the retarded, of which there are all too few . . . [Nancy] and
Bruce say that they do not expect Vicky to live with them for-
ever—any more than they expect the other children to.

She wonders aloud whether Vicky might help in some way
with little children. She is so good and capable with Cindy. Or,
Nancy speculates, Vicky might wash hair in a beauty shop. She
loves to play with hair and takes very good care of her own,

which falls softly almost to her shoulders, helping to hide the too-thick neck and too-thin ears that characterize mongoloids. Would it put people off, Nancy muses, to have Vicky wash their hair? Or maybe she could be an aide in a nursing home.

Meanwhile, Vicky at eleven lives very much in the present. No one would characterize her as a completely happy child, but then, is any eleven-year-old always completely happy? Her grandmother Humphrey tries very hard to distinguish between Vicky, eleven-year-old person, and Vicky, retarded child. Has she been weepy lately, while visiting the Humphreys in their summer home on Lake Waverly, because of some special, built-in frustrations of her affliction, or simply because she missed her sisters, or perhaps because she may be coming into puberty? It is hard to know.

Vicky can tear through the hallways of her house in Wayzata, Minnesota, naming the famous and the familiar in the photographs on the walls. . . .

Nancy finds her "stubborn" these days, another quality hard to evaluate in a child like Vicky, because retardation is sometimes accompanied by a kind of stick-to-itiveness and repetitiveness. If you ask Vicky to write her name, she will write and write and write with a kind of fierce concentration, and she will resist stopping. She does not always move easily from one activity, or tack, or concern, to another. Sometimes it is as if the needle has got stuck in the record and needs to be pushed on. It is difficult to tell when her stubbornness is an act of will.

She wants terribly much to be just like her sisters—especially like Jill, with whom she is very competitive. In another family this would be dismissed as just plain old sibling rivalry. For Vicky, however, it operates in special ways. On the one hand, it is probably true that her passion to be like Jill motivates her to learn; and when she can, as with swimming, it gives her enormous satisfaction. She is extremely proud of the gold medal she won in the Kennedy "special Olympics" for the retarded. On the other hand, when she can't keep up with her lithe, agile, articulate younger sister, and as the gap between them widens each year, it is especially frustrating to her.

On the whole, Nancy and Bruce treat Vicky in the same casual way that they do the other children. In the summer, she runs barefoot from the TV room, up through the kitchen and out the garage to the pool, following or followed by Jill and Amy and their friends, pausing to talk to a dog here, a cat there, or to watch a new guinea pig nibble some grass. She rides the horse at Waverly, goes to dancing class in her leotards, and last winter she learned to ice-skate. Her parents take her everywhere—to the supermarket, to church, on vacations. Yet her mother admits that even now she finds public stares hard to take, for although Vicky is quite pretty by any standards, she is still unmistakably mongoloid.

Nancy feels comfortable enough to be able to say to Vicky, as she does to Jill or Amy, "Where's your brain? What have you got up there—sawdust?" and Muriel Humphrey has learned to hold her tongue when Jills calls everyone in sight, including Vicky, "dummy." On the other hand, when Nancy caught Jill making fun of some of the children at Fraser, she lashed out at her with, "Suppose they all started making fun of you because of your big butt?"

Jill and Amy are aware that Vicky is different, but there is very little explicit discussion of her difference. Nancy says that telling Jill and Amy about Vicky has been like telling children about sex. You don't sit them down and tell them everything at once. You answer questions when they come up, and you tell them as much as you think they're ready to know. Vicky's difference does not seem to be a matter of any concern to Jill and Amy. Bruce thinks that Vicky might, at some later time, be a source of embarrassment to her younger sisters, but she certainly isn't now.

If, as much as possible, Vicky is treated like the others, there are still ways in which she cannot be, either for her own protection or for her mother's. Nancy is a young woman who has no taste for martyrdom. She admits, for example, to being "basically afraid" of retarded children other than Vicky. She would not know what to do if a child were to have a seizure, she says. She is used to Vicky's somewhat thick speech, which is improving with therapy, and understands her, but she doesn't know if she would understand another handicapped child. Vicky is predictable to her, another child is not. And so Vicky has never had a party other than family birthday parties. Only in recent months did she have a friend over to spend the night.

Nancy respects her own limitations as well as her daughter's. If she did not, she would not have managed these eleven years since Vicky's birth with such an absence of self-pity.

In another way, too, Vicky is treated differently, but that is of her own doing. Her grandfather Humphrey has remarked, "There is a strange brightness about her, and she literally soaks up love." Her grandmother Solomonson says, "She does something for everybody. We think of her as a blessing and a joy." Muriel Humphrey says that "Vicky makes us all stretch our capacities. She is a special child indeed, in that she is so specially loving and loved."

The frank discussion of their feelings about Vicky on the part of the members of her family make it possible to see the turmoil that the birth of a retarded child creates in a whole family. Guilt, a wish to fix blame on some other family member, worry about the future, strain on other children all occur in most families where there is a retarded child. The family described here, although nationally prominent and knowledgeable about many things, had needs no different from those of families in other walks of life faced with a similar situation. And they made use of human service workers who could help them to understand and accept as normal their own feelings of distress as well as to suggest alternative courses of action from which they could choose in accordance with their own circumstances and convictions.

On the other side of the coin, this account shows that in spite of retardation, a child may be a happy, attractive, and beloved member of a family. Human service workers need to keep in mind that retarded children are children, and retarded adults are people with many interesting characteristics, lovable and unlovable, differing from one another as all other human beings do. The more they are seen as individuals who happen to have some handicaps, and the more human service workers can help families to see them in this way, the more honest relationships can develop between them and other people.

child and family agency: jenny

Under what headings does a discussion of the human services as they relate to an unmarried mother belong? Should she be considered as a child, as a member of a family, as the head of a family, as a single working woman? Her child might be categorized as a child in his own home or he might become an adopted child or one in a foster home. Any one of these categories might be the right one for individual unmarried mothers and their children. Like all the other people discussed in this book, unmarried mothers must be considered as individuals in a particular setting at a particular time. Human services for them must take into account much more than the single fact that they are unmarried. But it is true that a teen-age girl, pregnant outside of marriage, has to face a number of problems which combine to make her life more difficult than any one of them would singly. Human service workers coming into contact with girls in this difficult situation need to respond to all of their needs, not only to the obvious ones related to pregnancy.

In the following excerpts from an account of work with a group of unmarried mothers, a highly experienced psychiatric social worker describes her observations in her work with them over a period of several years, as part of a project in a Southern state to help unmarried mothers complete their education, academic or vocational, and find their way to a personally satisfying life. The program consisted of meetings of a small group of girls and individual meetings and conferences with them and their families as seemed useful. It is notable that although this social worker was well qualified and experienced in helping people through clinical "one-to-one" interviewing, she chose chiefly to work with Jenny as a member of her family—as well as the head of her own—and to help her make use of the facilities, inadequate as they might be, of the community.

The social worker's understanding of Jenny's natural distrust of her as a white person influenced her manner of introducing herself and offering help. Throughout, she sought to understand Jenny's family, their special way of life, Jenny's relationships with others, the community both black and white, and to mobilize what she saw and heard on Jenny's behalf.

> Jenny, when I first met her, was a tall black girl of 16, obviously pregnant. She was caring for a neighbor's baby with accustomed ease and she admitted me with a silence that was neither hostile nor defensive. Several toddlers were sitting on the floor in front of the television—her three-year-old brother and children of two married sisters who lived nearby. In spite of a clutter of belongings, worn furniture, and a big gap in the ceiling plaster, there was a feeling of spaciousness. Jenny's response to the unexpected white visitor proved to be characteristic of her—silence until she felt certain and then significant remarks. Jenny has never had any small-talk. At two points in my explanation of the dropout project her face lighted up—help in securing further education and the prospect of group meeting now. In relation to exclusion from day school she said simply, "They say we're too mature." She told me that her best girl friend was also pregnant and found her name on my list. Both of them had been in the eleventh grade.
>
> In giving family data, Jenny, like many of the girls I inter-

Excerpts from "The Real World of the Negro Mother" by Beatrice S. Reiner, unpublished paper, n.d., pp. 3–5, 19, 21, 23–26. Used courtesy of the author.

viewed, made a point of being exact about surnames. In her case, her mother, 19-year-old sister, 7-year-old sister, and 3-year-old brother carried the name of Smith, while she and her 12-year-old sister were Browns. (Her mother's reversion to Smith after separation from Mr. Brown probably means that the fathers of the last two children were never part of the family.)

In answer to questions, she said she was receiving prenatal care from a Negro physician and that the father of the baby was not helping her. The main support of the family was her mother's day work. Two other facts came out—one of her married sisters had a secretarial job in the Negro community and her nineteen-year-old sister was attending junior college on a scholarship—both significant of higher than average educational standards.

Jenny's mother, who was seen later, was a thin, overburdened, worried-looking woman, still young and with ambitions for her children. When her cares piled up she would take a day off from work because she felt "nervous." The older daughter, Louise, also seemed anxiety-driven and later dropped out of college because of a psychosomatic illness. Mrs. Smith had great confidence in the Negro family physician and a good part of her earnings went to pay his fees. The maternal grandmother, who was seen once, was a dominating old lady who apparently had set up standards that her daughter tried vainly to perpetuate.

Jenny was in most ways the opposite of her sister Louise, with whom she carried on a running feud. Jenny was bigger, darker, and more reticent, giving an impression of calmness and latent strength. When the family was seen together it became obvious that Jenny was unique both in appearance and temperament. She confided ultimately that she was the image of her father and that in primary school the teachers would never believe that she was Mrs. Smith's daughter. . . . Unlike Louise, Jenny had little interest in academic subjects. In her first two years of high school she had enjoyed basketball and "got by" in courses. She had ambitions to study cosmetology or practical nursing. She was sensitive about being five feet eleven inches tall and having big feet. She was always uneasy if caught working around the house in old pants, and she would never come to meetings in working clothes, even if she was late.

Jenny was well-liked by her contemporaries. New recruits to the group always seemed reassured when they heard that she was a member, although some of them told her that when they first met her they had thought her unfriendly. Once Jenny's initial silence had passed, her response was genuine, reliable and often humorous, but after any lapse of time there had to be another warming up period. Her observation was acute and her judgment apt to be sound.

Jenny had dated the father of her baby for seven months before her only experience of intercourse, during which conception occurred. In this she seemed to be unique, since most of the girls had had frequent relations with a boy for a year or more before pregnancy. She indicated that she could have married the boy, but she obviously thought he was unreliable, and he never did help her. . . .

[After her baby was born] Jenny's mother laid down strict rules for Jenny to follow with the baby and Jenny was afraid to deviate from them, though she did not trust them entirely. . . .

That summer was taken up with the girls' attempts to qualify for MDTA courses or some other education. This meant many trips by the girls to the State Employment Service where they became caught in the confusion caused by a deluge of applicants and conflicting directives. The girls already had a deep distrust of the Service, not readily verbalized but implicit in their not going there except as a last resort. They believed that the State Employment Service would think they were no good for anything but domestic jobs, which they dreaded because they were poorly paid and required adaptation to the whims of unpredictable women. The girls went to the Employment Service expecting a runaround and their worst fears were fulfilled . . . but after several of them had been given the same tests twice and no precautions seemed to prevent confusions, I began to share their distrust. While they sat and waited in the employment office they were keenly aware of white youngsters who seemed to be getting different treatment. . . .

[Eventually, Jenny was accepted for "nurse's aide."]

Unexpectedly, Jenny did not take the MDTA course in September. She had taken a job in a cafeteria. . . . Having recently moved the family to more sanitary up-to-date housing (but more crowded) Mrs. Smith felt pressure for money and made Jenny feel guilty for adding a baby to the family. Afterwards Mrs. Smith reverted again to her regret that Jenny was not being prepared for a better job.

Jenny made the best of her decision and expressed enthusiasm about earning more money and working with other young people who provided her with gossip. But as time went on, she began to refer to her delayed anger after numerous occasions when she was pressured to give extra money to her mother or to the younger children. In a few months she changed jobs, working in a grocery store near home, so that she could go to night school. She went for only a few weeks and then began to work longer hours because her mother's AFDC check had been cut from $81.00 to $38.00 on the strength of Jenny's earning $21.00 a week.

In February Jenny suddenly rented a furnished cottage next to Julie's and moved there with Diana, who was now thirteen months old. Jenny told her mother that she had to live her own life. Mrs. Smith was upset, seemingly more for herself than for Jenny, but she did make it clear that Jenny was still one of the family. Jenny had saved money for the first week's rent, eighteen dollars, the electric deposit and a tank of cooking gas, had collected bedding and utensils from her employer and friends, and had asked her father for some help. She had a struggle to manage on $33.00 a week, but contrary to everyone's predictions, she "made it" and remained there for several months until Julie's mother took a whole second floor in a frame building and Jenny moved in with them. Julie cared for Diana, who responded to more consistent care, becoming more outgoing and less awkward in her movements. She was a large child who had seemed somewhat uncoordinated. Jenny's expressed ambition now reverted to taking training for practical nursing when she became eighteen.

In December Jenny returned to her mother's home because of a severe bladder infection that kept her from working. In the meantime, her sister had married, but the house was still crowded because her grandmother had moved in.

After Julie was married a short time later, Jenny announced her plans for her own wedding in the spring to a friend of Julie's husband. She seemed happy about it but said cautiously that she hoped it would work out all right. The plans were interrupted by her fiance's probation officer. Jenny had not been aware that he had been "in a little trouble" and she broke off with him. Later that spring she moved into an apartment of her own with Diana, but began to have skin eruptions on her hands that the doctor could not explain. She admitted that she felt discouraged and that she probably was not eating the right food. All her life she had been unable to eat breakfast and she usually ate very little lunch. She said now that she would probably never marry and she thought that she could get along without men. In the meantime, she had had four different jobs. She lost the one in the grocery store because of an argument with the white owner who suspected her of knowing who broke into another store in the neighborhood. Then she worked with Lucy at the retirement home until her illness. After that she worked as a short order cook and salad girl in a small motel restaurant until the end of the tourist season when she was laid off. She was now working in a neighborhood restaurant, and wondering whether to apply to the Women's Job Corps or look for some other kind of training. . . .

The only question about the Job Corps is Diana. It is easy to say that the family would take care of her. Jenny knows this is true but she is hesitant. Diana is fond of her grandmother but Jenny is Diana's mother both in fact and feeling.

There are clear indications that the experienced professional social worker who organized the group Jenny belonged to could see herself as the girls might see her and could accept the necessity of taking the time to let them learn to trust her good intentions. She was well aware of the fact that at first she seemed to them yet another faceless white person who would at best exploit them and at worst shame and injure them. They had no experience with white people who behaved otherwise. The social worker knew that she would set off alarm systems in Jenny and the other girls and that she could not avoid doing this in the initial contacts. One consequence of this understanding was to plan to make the first contact by visiting the girls in their own homes where they might be expected to feel most comfortable and secure, rather than sending a written invitation to a meeting in an impersonal location. In this way, the social worker signaled her willingness to try to understand and help without having to put it into words which might have fallen on deaf ears. If she had not understood the possible effect of her own color, she might well have decoded Jenny's initial silence as indifference, both to her pregnancy and to the social worker's offer to try to help.

But here, as in many other relationships made by human service workers, the fact that the girls came to accept the worker did not mean that they would now continue to do so and conform to the standards of society. If the social worker had protested Jenny's many changes of job and plans, some made at considerable cost of time and effort by the social worker, Jenny might well have slipped back into familiar attitudes of distrust of white people. By her willingness to accept the way Jenny lived, her steadfast maintenance of their relationship, and her willingness to see Jenny's difficulties from Jenny's point of view, the social worker was able to continue to help Jenny work her way through one of the most difficult and distressing situations that a woman can face—the reconciliation of the personal needs of an adolescent girl with her role as a mother and her love of her child whom she had to support both in a realistic and an emotional sense.

One field of service that has developed very rapidly in the last few years is that of care for the aged. Where once older people were cared for in the homes of their relatives, today many of them are residents of special facilities, some of which are oriented toward older people who no longer wish the responsibility of maintaining independent residences, others toward those who need physical care and who may or may not have financial resources. Many human service workers—nurse's aides, orderlies, trained nurses, physiotherapists, social workers—are likely to be found in nursing homes. Should the individuals found in these facilities be included in this chapter on services to families when, in fact, they are living apart from their families and are not directly cared for by them? The decision to include them in this chapter was made because to the older people themselves, their family status is still a very important one. For many, their presence in the facility for the care of the aged is a symbol of their changed family status—from that of the head of a family, responsible for caring for others, to that of a child for whom plans are made and carried out.

It would be wrong to assume that families who do not care for their elderly relatives at home are callous and unloving. When there were no alternatives to home care life was not always ideal for older people. Many were unhappy at the burden they became to younger relatives, at the loss of privacy, and the strains of constant contact with younger generations. Trends toward smaller living quarters, social insurance support, and increased longevity, all suggest that the field of care for the elderly is one of the human services which will continue to expand and to engage human service workers at many levels.

nursing home for the aged: leab

Leab, the central character in a modern novel, is both an individual and a typical example of a nursing home resident, although the home selected for him by his affluent and affectionate family is unquestionably more comfortable and considerate than many others. This description of him affords the reader some insights into the thoughts and feelings of those to be met in the human services for older people and their families.

Look: here is Leab, an old man in bed. The night is ending, the first gray light of dawn softens the blackness of the room. Leab has suffered through a restless night, and now, not quite asleep, not yet awake, he lies stretched out along the diagonal of a bed that is as rumpled as his thick white hair. The blanket is twisted at his feet; the sheet is untucked and wadded beneath him; the pillow hovers a moment, then tumbles to the floor; he has even managed to unsettle the mattress, which sits askew upon the box spring. Somewhere someone flushes a toilet; outside a few sparrows twitter; an automobile whispers over asphalt and is gone.

Solomon Leab, 67 years old, a big paunchy bear of a man, poet, philosopher, skeptic, schoolteacher (retired: June 31, 1965), an ugly man despite his broad forehead and ruddy cherublike cheeks. His tangle of white hair has a taint of yellow in it like a polar bear's pelt; beneath his chin his wrinkled flesh forms crevices in which whitish stubble grows; his massive eyebrows are black, as are the hairs that sprout like jungle-weed from his nostrils and ears. His nose is protuberant, his lips fat and pendulous; a face grown increasingly grotesque with age. And yet it is easy to imagine small children finding his face attractive, clambering up onto his lap to grasp at his earlobes and lips, pulling and poking at his face as though it were a great mass of putty, screaming with delight whenever they managed to sculpt a new expression into it. . . .

Look about: Leab's room is small and simply furnished; the dim light, dulling the walls' bright peach paint, makes it seem drab. There are seventeen more rooms just like it: each has its bed, its night table, its dresser, its Renoir or Degas reproduction, its musty odor, its peach walls—peach having been chosen, gerontologically, to cheer up the old folk. This is the Sunnyside Home for the Aging.

Built before the Depression to house the noted financier, Simon B. Malstein, Sunnyside offers golden-agers the most up-to-date comfort, care, and recreation available in the Greater New York area. Private rooms, a half-acre garden, eight asso-

From *Make Yourself an Earthquake* by Mark Dintenfass (Boston: Little, Brown and Co., 1969), pp. 1–6. Copyright © 1969 by Mark Dintenfass. Reprinted with the permission of the publisher and Monica McCall, IFA.

ciated geriatric specialists, and a modern kitchen providing kosher cuisine are just a few of Sunnyside's attractions. . . .

The children of the neighborhood hold it in awe, as they might a haunted house. In the spring, when the old people sun themselves in the garden, the children gather at the fence to gawk, perhaps believing that here are the ghosts—the proprietors have put them out to air.

Often Leab would sit in the garden and gawk right back at the children, wondering if they ever considered, the brats, that young and old alike were made of the same stuff. At first, when he was still recovering from the attack, the children would make him sad. . . .

But return: consider the sunrise, flaming in the east. Hours before it blazed in Africa; it set the Atlantic on fire; now it turns the gray buildings of the City to purple—often Leab had watched the sun rise and thought such thoughts, first with ambition, later with despair, now with a new longing. Ridiculous, of course, to think the Home a prison, his room a cell. But still—. . . .

At this time of morning, a few months earlier, Nurse would have come in to wash him, shave him, and feed him breakfast. In those days Leab believed he was dying, that there was nothing left in him but dry rot. Now, remembering, he felt a sense of urgency. He went to the mirror and looked at himself. His hands were trembling slightly, and he glanced down at them with disgust.

A confluence of events plunged Leab into senescence—before he had considered himself middle-aged at worst. After 35 years teaching English at Midwood High in Brooklyn, he had been retired. Then, a few weeks later, his wife, Sheba (not her real name, but he always called her that: Solomon and Sheba: one of those silly things that happen in marriage), Sheba had turned yellow. Liver cancer: she did not linger long. And then, shortly after the funeral, Leab, sitting in a movie theater, feeling sorry for himself, had the attack. It was as though someone had slammed a sledgehammer into his left side, the hammerhead smashing ribs and organs, and then sticking there. Massive coronary occlusion, the doctors called it. Leab remembered pain, an oxygen tent, needles, then a long period of unconsciousness filled with dreams. Bed rest was prescribed. ("You see, the blood must find new pathways.") That winter of convalescence his hands had begun to tremble. He could not control the trembling, could not make fists of his hands.

That's when Leab despaired. When his children brought him books or magazines, he claimed he could not read them, that the print was nothing but a blur. He convinced himself he was losing his memory, and spent hours writing down trivial recollections. There were times when he refused to get out of bed at all, saying he was too weak and wanted only to be left alone. He felt pains the doctors could not diagnose, and began to believe he had caught Sheba's cancer. They couldn't talk him out of it. Morning, afternoon, and evening he would study his face in the mirror, searching his eye-whites and skin for signs of jaundice. At his worst moments he believed he was going to die in just a few weeks, and that his children, the doctors, the nurses, and all the old people in the Home had entered into a conspiracy to keep the truth from him.

But when spring came a year ago a remarkable change began to take place. Leab decided he wasn't going to die after all. He wasn't even senile. His hands trembled simply because he was still alive and not using up the stuff of life that remained in him. It was all excess energy.

So he began again to be active and soon discovered that the more he tried to wear himself out, the more energetic he felt. Before he had almost no appetite, and had begun to shrivel; now he was almost constantly hungry. He would awaken in the middle of the night, sneak down to the pantry, and gorge himself on bread and butter. Soon the doctors started cautioning him about the dangers of obesity.

The sight of the old people dying around him, the mere thought of death, seemed to set his glands to work. Adrenaline flowed and he felt young. It wasn't long before he realized the Home could no longer contain him. But when he talked with his children about leaving, they smiled, they just smiled.

It is notable that even in this geriatic facility so unusually well staffed with experts, and with the continuing interest of his family, Leab has become a stereotype—an old person in a home for old people, a convalescent from acute coronary disease. No one takes into account that he is still a *person* growing and changing through life experience and that he is today not the same person who came into the home a dependent invalid. The many well-trained and well-intentioned human service workers failed to see the change in him and neither heard nor attempted to decode the signals he was sending about his needs to reenter the mainstream of life, to continue to be an individual not just a member of a large group labeled "the elderly." In the novel, Leab takes matters into his own hands to reestablish himself in the world of active, living people, "runs away" from the home and joins in the adventures of a young niece which lead, inevitably, to his death. It is a more satisfactory end for him than years of half life in the safe comfort of the home would have been.

ex-migrant family:
rita fernandez

Some families are strangers in their own country. Speaking a foreign language and living in a foreign culture, they are often treated as though their differences were bad or as if they themselves were invisible. Only very recently have the human services attempted to help Mexican-American families to full participation in American life. In an interview at the Community College she was attending, Rita Fernandez talked about herself and her family, their loyalties and ambitions.

RITA: We came here, and my dad worked in the field and all of us worked in the summers, and then it happened—he had an operation, a hernia, and he came down with asthma really bad— and then diabetes. And he was mad at my mother because she made him come here from Texas because of the money—and better schools she heard. And so, here we were and didn't know what to do.

INTERVIEWER: How old were you?

R: I was—12—11—I think. This lady and her church, they really helped us that winter, I can remember. They brought food and they brought quilts and things like this. I don't know who it was that said that we could get some help—go to the Welfare and they could help. And this was quite hard because, you know, this was the first time we had been on Welfare. My dad always had a job. You're criticized, you know, for being on Welfare. Even Mexican-Americans. People go on Welfare and they criticize them.

I: Why?

R: Because they say that—well, they think—you're on Welfare because you don't want to work. And I can remember because I was kind of—I told that man who came up to the house from the Welfare. We don't want your help, I said. We're willing to work, me and my brother—we'll work.

From an unpublished tape interview.

I: Are you the oldest?

R: No, I have an older brother. We don't need your help, I said. . . .

I: Can your father work at all now?

R: No, he can't.

I: That's hard for him.

R: Yeah, and he wants to, you know, but—and also it's really bad because they look down on you.

I: How did you get to this college?

R: Oh, I dropped out of high school, to get them out of the Welfare. I liked school, and I never was discriminated from the whites, as to my race, being Mexican-American. I imagine because I was kind of shy and just didn't talk to them. Maybe this was why I wasn't discriminated, I don't know. And they really didn't treat you bad. There was just me and my brothers and our families and we enjoyed going to school there. But I dropped out of school in the ninth grade. I dropped out of school and I got a job—I had to, you know—I got a job and I started to work. All I wanted was to provide things for my family. And it's kind of funny, because in a way I found out that I couldn't do very much. Because what jobs could I get? There really wasn't much that I could do. And I said, well, what am I going to do? So I thought, well, maybe if I go back to school and I get my GED and I get an education, maybe that way I'll be able to provide more, help them more. And so what I did is I asked a man who was working for this organization that helps Mexican-Americans to obtain their GED or stuff like this. . . . I told him that I'd like to come back to school and work for my GED or get in some kind of program that will help me to get an education. So he said, well, how old are you? And I said, I'm seventeen. And he said, well, then there is a program. What you do is work as an aide in whatever you want to be. And I said, well, I think I'll be a secretary. I think that would be the most easy thing that I could be, because it wouldn't take so much education. And he said, well, OK then, I'll refer you to the office where you will work as an aide and the lady will teach you how to type and teach you the office procedures and help you. She will be your supervisor. And you will be paid $1.75 an hour and actually what you'll be doing, you'll be learning and working at the same time. And I said, fine, I'll go along with that. So, in the meantime, you're supposed to go to some night classes and get your GED. So I said OK. So I went to that agency and was working, but as it turned out, my supervisor really didn't care that much. She really never actually took the time to tell me, you know, to teach me. At that time the office was run by just whites. It wasn't run by Mexican-Americans, and that was why—

Anyway, what happened then, my parents had to go to Mexico in an emergency. They had to, because my grandmother was ill, and they thought she was going to die. They asked me to come along because they said I could help my dad to get there. Direct him, read the signs, and stuff like this. I said OK, I'll ask permission. I went in and talked to her, and she said, no, I'm sorry, you can't go. You have to stay here. And I said I'm going to go anyway because my folks need me. Well, she said, if you leave, you know, you won't be able to get into it at all. And I really got mad, but then later I said, well I don't care. I'm just going—they need me. Anyway, she got very upset and she called the boss. She told the boss I wasn't obeying her, that I would like to go on my own without her permission. So I didn't care anyway—I left.

So finally when I came back, she had resigned and they told me, you can work here and after you get your GED, we'll try to find a job for you. So I did. I worked there and then I got my GED and then they got a job for me. There were five men and I was the only girl in this office, and they were really very nice. My boss knew I didn't know very much, but he really kind of helped me. Once he gave me some minutes that he wanted me to type and of course I'd never typed any minutes before, so I didn't know how so then he told me, he showed me a copy of some other minutes that had been typed before and I kind of followed this and I know I kept lousing it up 'cause I wasn't such a good typist. Here I was, sometimes I'd go type a page all fine and all of a sudden I'd leave out a section, you know. It was kind of boring, too, in a way, because there wasn't much to do. The phone hardly ever rang. Most of the time I'd just sit there and read a magazine or something, or dust around. So finally I told my boss I'm kind of bored here, and I don't have that much to do. I think I'll go back and try to work in the cannery because there really isn't much to do. And I told my mom, and my mom said, you must be stupid, you know, because here you're leaving a job to go to work at the cannery. And I told her, the cannery was paying more, and that's the other reason I went there. So I left there and went to work at the cannery. It was kind of fun 'cause here were more Mexican-Americans I could just talk to them.

Then after that season there I was again without a job. This is when I went to work at the mushroom plant. I lied about my age, told them I was eighteen when actually I was only seventeen. So when I was working there I fell down and I hurt myself. I wasn't terribly hurt, but I hurt my side and my dad said no, you're not going back there again, you know. So I left that job.

Then I heard that there was positions opening for teachers' aides at the organization that helps Mexican-Americans for the winter adult school. And I asked if I could do it. They said just help the teacher. You don't have a class of your own, you just help them out in different sections. So then, fine, OK, I was going to try it anyway. I went in there and the first day I went I was all nervous and everything, you know. And it turned out that I got a class of my own, because there weren't enough teachers around. It was a pretty large one. There were eight or nine students there. And the first day I asked one of the teachers exactly where they were, what books they were using and all this. And she told me and then I sat down and really in this area, here the students were just learning like the ABC's and different things like this. So I started with the ABC's.

I: Were most of these migrant workers?

R: Yes, Mexican-American, you know, so I started with the ABC's and it was kind of hard because although they spoke English enough to get the point across, they couldn't read and they couldn't even say the ABC's. I really enjoyed it. It was kind of my fault that they didn't learn as much as they could have. This is really what inspired me into teaching.

Mr. F. from the Community College used to come over and he said to me, would you like to be a teacher? I kind of looked at him blank, you know. I said, oh, I don't know, because I don't think I can do it. He says, oh, I think you can. So anyway, I kept that in mind and after the program terminated, then I gave him a ring and I told him, I think I will take up teaching and what will I need. And he said, well, come over and we'll take a look at the college and then take a look at the outline and the classes that you've got to take and the schedule. So they put me in a couple of prep classes like fundamentals of algebra and fundamentals of speech, and a few that would prepare me in reading and would prepare me for college. But I was kind of anxious. I wanted to start off right away, so I took some sociology classes, you know. I wasn't prepared for it, but I took my test for a C—I was kind of lucky, I guess.

And from then on, of course, I went to summer school and then after summer school I finished the year, then I told them I was going to work for the summer. My counselor said—she was kind of helping me and saying, you know, you should go on to school and continue. And she really did inspire me. I was really kind of glad for it. But then I told her, no, I think I'd better work and get some money. So I went to work at the cannery and after that I came back. And now I have got a scholarship for the last two years of college.

This is for a bi-lingual program and means I'll be working for a certificate in elementary major, and I'll be minoring in bilingual education. And I think I'll get my tuition and my board and room paid, except for my books.

I: Do you like to teach?

R: Yes, but sometimes I really doubt. Will I be able to do it? Like for instance, I've got a science teacher—he does his best, I know that, but he's unable to reach the students. The students are left blank—can't get it. And as I look at some of the teachers I think I might be in this same position, because I imagine it's kind of hard to get something across to students—into their level where they can get it. Some are smart, while others are slow learners and takes them twice as long to get something. And this is the thing that I wish that I could do—be a good teacher, put things across so that they can get it.

I: I think you'd be very good with children. Aren't you?

R: I hope so, I wasn't very bright or anything, but I got B's and C's and a couple of A's and I was proud of my grades, but the fact that there were some—since in most schools I was about the only Mexican-American, I could notice that there were some—whites who had problems, and they were picked on by other Americans and they would mistreat them in a way and it made me mad in a way. It was their own race, you know. Actually I keep in mind that this problem exists for everybody, not only us.

I: How does it exist among Mexican-Americans?

R: Oh, it exists in a way that perhaps there's lighter colors or there's darker. Some are Mexican Indians and some are Spanish, more Spanish in them you see. They say, so I'm better than you, you see.

I: Which is better than which?

R: The Spanish than the Indians. I often got along better with the whites than I did with the Mexican-Americans because they kind of discriminated me because I was Indian, Mexican-American Indian.

I: I should think that would be the best thing to be.

R: It is now—I'm proud of what I am, but before I kind of

didn't want to admit what I was, because, you know, discrimination, but now I'm proud. I'm really proud of what I am.

I: How did you get to be proud?

R: Oh because my brother was proud. He didn't care. I know he'd come up and he'd say, well I'm an Indian. He never associated with Mexican-Americans. He'd say I'm an Indian. And I'm proud of what I am. And I know he kind of associated more with Americans—the whites, the cavachos, you know. Like some—not all Mexican-Americans, but there's some—just because you mix along with whites, they consider you're trying to Americanize yourself.

I: What does he do?

R: Him? He was a—what he did—he went to vocational school and learned a little bit of trade of mechanic. I guess I kind of learned from him a little bit. You've got to be proud of what you are, because nothing is going to change it. Just because you deny it, just because you try to speak just English, or dress just like this, it isn't going to change. The only fact that will turn out better is to admit and be proud of what you are. And try to better it.

I: Oh, but there's a lot to be proud of, in what you are.

R: Sure, that's just it! There is. There's so much. But you don't know, because you get the discrimination. You think, well, there isn't. You consider yourself inferior. That's just the point. Because you're discriminated, because you're considered inferior, well there isn't anything we should be proud of. But after a while you learn that there is. There is so much. You know that you can be proud of your culture. . . .

I know that bi-lingual education is important. Because here you're going to be taught a new culture—your culture—and you can be proud of it. When I was going to school in Texas you were forbidden to speak Spanish. You get punished for speaking Spanish. You see, as soon as you entered, got into the school grounds, you would leave whatever you were and you were in a world of whites and you had to be like them, you see. And now I think with bi-lingual education you're going to get a background of your culture and what it is. I don't know anything about my culture, the little bit that maybe Dad—as far as the history who were Mexico's heroes and things like this, what did they do, and as much as the background of Mexican-Americans, I don't know that because they never taught you these things. But, now many people are against bi-lingual education because they say that this will be an extra load for the Americans. Well, I don't know why many Caucasians are against it. Somebody said to me, well, what are you trying to do now, change the laws to suit you? It's just that we want to learn about ourselves, who we are, and what we can do, I guess.

In my mother's village, they still have their customs, you know. It's in Mexico. It's very small. There's a lake surrounded by villages, and the next village is a little more advanced than my mother's because they've got tap water, not inside. They've still got adobe houses but now they're painted. And most of the women there wear regular clothes, not short, but they don't wear the costumes any more. There are a lot of people who are going to school and they don't live there, they go to school and they only come home for the weekends and times of holidays. Where my mom lived, they're still less advanced than the other because they still wear the costumes and they still speak a lot of their native language. And there's quite a few illiterates still. They have some who are going to school and who have gotten their teaching degree or something, and then they leave. And there's only a few—as a matter of fact the teachers they usually have there are not from their own little village. They're from other villages. And there's a little area there—the different dialects of Tarasco Indians—but sometimes the dialects change, so here you have different little villages surrounding this lake. The ones up ahead don't speak the language anymore and they're trying to get away, mixing more with the Mexicans or the Spanish. So they're leaving the culture. And here you still have the fiestas. I don't know the history. I wish I did. They have what they call a patron and he's in the church in the village. They celebrate—I guess it must be his birthday—in November. They have this big fiesta. They've got bands that come. They choose a queen. I've never been to the fiesta and now with school I can't go. They don't have to have costumes because they always wear their costumes. But they wear fancier. Instead of the ordinary green and red they wear a fancy black wool skirt.

I: When did you leave Mexico?

R: I never lived in Mexico. I lived in Texas. And in '67 and '68 I went there. And that was because my grandmother died, and then my grandfather was ill.

I: What do you speak at home?

R: We speak Spanish and with many English words. My dad speaks Spanish. He came here in 1942, because he said he wanted to get into the war but they wouldn't let him in because he couldn't speak English. And so he has been here since then. And my mother came over in 1946. And my dad of course was a *bracero*—this is what they call farm workers. Farmers bring them over and they can work while there's work here and then they go back. My father was a bracero and you get a little card which is free admittance to here. And that came afterwards, though, because he said before there really wasn't that much concern about having papers. Anybody could cross the border. Later, I think it was around the '50's, they started the papers. Because my folks—they're not citizens—but they've got a passport. They really didn't get their passports until 1956. And my dad worked here and then he would go back. And then my mom came here and they stayed here. They were here illegally. Then when the United States really started trying to enforce it so there wouldn't be so much going back and forth, that's when the farmers which my dad worked for kind of kept them illegally. They couldn't go out much because they were afraid they'd catch 'em. They did go back to Mexico a couple of times and they'd come back again. My mother—you know she'd never give up. My dad had a card, it was no problem with him, but my mom, you know, whenever she knew she was pregnant she came back here because she wanted us to be a citizen, even though she was here illegally. And she kept coming back. And so I think it was in 1956 they got their passports. And they are here legally now. My dad never really wanted to become an American. He wanted to work here and go back to Mexico. Well, mom says, what are you going to do? The children they've got to have some place. They're citizens and I want them to get an education. My dad says, well OK if you want to—you go by yourself and I'll go back to Mexico. My mom says, oh no, you've got to come here. And so finally they stayed. The farmer my dad worked for was really nice because he helped my mom and my dad. He paid about two-thirds for the cost of their passports. So he was a real nice gentleman. But then he died and his sons took over—and they weren't like their father. My dad had the job there, but it wasn't the same. Then more people came in and it was a colony. When we left they had the braceros on one side and the families, who were citizens or had passports, on the other side. The braceros came only for the season and then they go back to Mexico until the next season. And we were given housing and of course, my dad was paid only the salary, but we had free rent, free electricity and free everything, so it really wasn't too bad. But my mother, she wanted to come to a place where we could make more money.

I: Is she pleased with what you're doing now?

R: Oh yes, yes. I told her that I got a scholarship. And first she says she won't let me. No, you're going to go too far and I won't let you leave so far away from home. But then my dad said, no, let her get it, so then she said OK, I guess you can live 300 miles from us.

I: Are there younger ones in your family that are coming along, too?

R: Oh yes, except for one, that's my 19-year-old brother. He had problems in school. He never could learn. It wasn't because of our language barrier, it was that he would not apply himself. If he could get away with it, he didn't study or if he could just be passed on to another grade without really working at it he was not concerned. I tried to tell him—don't do it; don't drop out. You're going to feel sorry. But he wasn't about to take my advice. So he just dropped out this last year. Now he is working in the fields. He has a job during the season, works in a cannery, gets good money, you know. He can't work in any other place because he doesn't have that education. But my little brother, he's really interested in school and he's been pretty good, too. He's a sopho- more. He wants to finish high school and then go into data proc- essing or something. I've got another sister who does well in school and she will keep on going to school. And then I still got another brother. He's slow at learning. He just can't pick up things. Still he goes to school and he hasn't done anything about dropping out. He comes with his report cards, a couple of D's and a couple of C's. And I told him, you got to work a little bit harder, you can do it, you know. It's a matter that you sit down and study. It's not that you're dumb or you can't. . . . And he looks at me and says, OK. Like last night I was telling him—he came with a report card and it says something like he's too shy, he isn't able to talk like in a group. And I told him, now don't be like that. I know what you're going through because I did the same thing. And I was kind of afraid, maybe if I say something, it's going to be a stupid thing and everybody will laugh at me and consider I'm stupid. And if I keep my mouth shut at least they won't know what's in my head. They may think I'm smart or something. So I told him you've got to speak up, but first you've got to read your work. Because how can you discuss something if you don't read your work? And so you've got to read and no matter how stupid it seems, you go to the teacher and say I don't know the definition for this word. I don't understand this phrase here. Just tell me what's going on there, or get the dictionary. I told him I live with the dictionary in my hand all the time. When I read it takes me twice as long as what others would do, because of my vocabulary. I look them up and I write them down and try to use them in a way, too. I told him, so I know exactly how you feel in a classroom but the thing is, don't think of other people, just come up and raise your hand and just try to discuss with them. But the thing is to prepare yourself, because if you're not prepared there isn't anything you can contribute to the class, if you haven't read your material.

I: What will you be teaching—little children or—?

R: Elementary from first to sixth is what I hope. But I've got one brother, he's only ten years old and he's in the fifth grade and he's getting along very good. B's and A's, wow! He's the smart one in the family. And I encourage him and I'll give him a dollar or something, if he gets good grades. And I remember the other day this girl said, well, that's not right—because you're bribing him. But I told her, I want him to know that I really appreciate that he's working hard for it. And he's doing well. When he was little, I told my mother we got to speak English. We've got to teach him English and the alphabet and we've got to teach him the numbers before he goes to school, because we know exactly what it'll be like because we went through it, too. So we speak to him in English and we teach him the alphabet. So when he went to school for the first grade he knew English a little, not much, but a little. That was to get him on his way. We're doing the same thing with my five-year-old brother. He knows the ABC's now and he can count up to fifteen and he still is working on the pronunciation and the sounds of the letters. Now that I'm away, my younger sister, the one that's in the eighth grade, she helps him, too. She will sit down with him and teach him, so he can just go in there and be one step ahead. Because you go in there without a word of English and it takes you about the whole year to finally know what they're talking about. And this is what I think is really good about bi-lingual education, because here a student will go in there who can't speak any English at all and you'll tell them, well this is a house, in Spanish, and they know the Spanish so they can just relate both of them, and they know what the teacher's talking about.

Rita came into contact from her earliest years with a succession of human service workers, some who saw only an impassive brown face and heard only the broken English of a non-American child of whom little could be expected. Others saw a girl trying hard to help her family and to maintain her identity as a member of an ethnic group while she longed for the success and acceptance that assimilation into the majority culture could bring her. Rita's struggle to remain a close member of her family, helping them financially and otherwise, and to achieve the independence from them that would allow her to become herself is the struggle of all adolescents. It is greatly complicated by the tradition of the ethnic society in which she has grown up and from which she has derived her values. It might be noted, too, that the community college teacher who recognized Rita's talent did not urge her to forsake her family as the secretary, her first supervisor, had done. Instead, he gave her time and encouragement to discover her own special bent and talent.

Rita's story may also help human service workers, such as the welfare worker, to understand why people who have asked for badly needed help may then make the worker the object of open hostility when he tries to give it. Most human service workers will meet families like the Fernandez—first generation immigrants from a foreign culture—as they have since the beginning of organized human services. It is important for them to appreciate that their difficulties stem, not from ignorance, lack of intelligence, or ambition but from the struggle to reconcile the demands of two different cultures in a way which will allow them freedom to develop as a people, proud of their heritage and able to function in both worlds.

This chapter may be bewildering and depressing because it demonstrates that a human service worker with families—and many who work with individuals with family ties—must take into consideration not only the individual himself but the many points of contact he has with other family members. The human service worker cannot expect to know, much less to influence all these subtle interrelationships. He may wonder how much he can hope to help any one person who is at the same time responding to so many other influences. He can take some comfort in recognizing, on the other hand, that when he is able to bring about some change toward happier, more successful functioning in one member of a family—Mrs. Brown for example—it will positively influence many other people. What is perhaps most important in working with families is to make note of what can be learned about all the family members, to consider individuals' interactions as well as the family as a whole unit in interaction with the larger social group of which it is a part. Perhaps such a long-range view will give the human service worker the perspective he needs. He will recognize that though it is not an easy task, it is possible to bring about positive change when the larger picture is kept in sight.

questions

Although she might not have realized it, the homemaker had an unusually well-tuned system for giving and receiving signals, coded and uncoded. List as many of these signals as you can, noting her response to them, verbal and nonverbal.

Mr. and Mrs. Brown, though beset by serious problems since early childhood, had apparently had little contact with human service workers except for Mrs. Brown's brief stay in a foster home and Mr. Brown's long hospitalization. How might they have been helped if their difficulties had been observed earlier and their silent cries for help answered?

If you were the human service worker connected with Vicky's school, would you urge her mother to see that Vicky had more social contacts with other retarded children and if so how would you do it?

If Leab's family and the staff at the home for the elderly had been more observant and had really seen and listened to Leab, how might they have helped him without jeopardizing his life?

additional reading

LeMasters, E. E. *Parents in Modern America.* Homewood, Ill.: Dorsey Press, 1970. Written in an informal style, this book discusses the changes that have come about in American families over the past generation and describes the relationships of parents with their children, with each other, and with the community about them. All kinds of parents are portrayed—foster parents, adoptive parents, and stepparents; the final chapter describes the varieties of counseling that are available to parents. The book contains many references to other volumes on behavioral science and frequently it offers comments that can help the human service worker to decide which field he will pursue.

Dybwad, Gunnar. *Challenges in Mental Retardation.* New York: Columbia University Press, 1964. This is a collection of speeches and writings of a former director of national and international organizations for improving the lot of the mentally retarded of all ages. While it is not quick and easy reading, it offers the human service worker a broad view of what is being done at present and how much remains to be done in a rapidly developing and important field of service. The advantages and disadvantages of institutionalization are discussed, and there are many stimulating comparisons of services for the mentally retarded in many countries.

Coles, Robert, M.D. *Children of Crisis: a Study of Courage and Fear.* Boston: Little, Brown and Co., 1967. "My job has been to learn what I can about individuals contending with a series of social crises. I brought with me a particular kind of training—the child psychiatrist's—and my purpose was to put that training to use as effectively as possible under conditions rather unlike those usually obtaining in clinical practice." That is the author's modest statement about this moving book about the effect on black and white people of the first steps in the desegregation of public schools in the South. It offers the human service worker an intimate acquaintance with some of the most and some of the least admirable people he will ever have the opportunity to get to know through the compassionate eyes of a highly trained professional in close contact with them over a long, stressful period. It may provide him with an object lesson not only in the value to be gained from a painstaking effort to understand a complex signal system but in the way a human service worker may influence the lives of people in crisis by "being there," by genuine concern, empathy, and acceptance of attitudes and actions which may be far from conforming with his personal standards. Although it deals with a special population, it is really a book about families of all kinds in many settings and will offer the human service worker much food for thought, even if it is not read in its entirety.

7 | the human service worker and the community

All the human services have three objectives: to prevent the development of problems which will handicap people; to help people solve the problems that they have; and to prevent people from succumbing to difficulties which threaten to overwhelm them. Most human services offer some or all these things in different settings with the use of some variation of helping methods.

For many years, human service workers in the community were found either assisting the privileged sectors of society who were interested in organizing themselves to support services for the less fortunate, or in settlement houses and similar agencies in the overcrowded, poor sections of large cities where waves of immigrants from Europe and rural America had come in search of the "promised land." Jane Addams and other settlement leaders believed that they could help best if they moved into these neighborhoods themselves, learned what the residents there most needed and wanted, and helped them to get it. They encouraged the people to acquire education, they provided a wide range of recreational activities for children from crowded homes, and they fought for better housing, play space, and fair employment, both on behalf of their neighbors and as partners with them. They encouraged the organization of groups of people who preferred to contribute money instead of services and kept these groups informed about the conditions which needed remedying.

The settlement movement was on the whole successful for many individuals who were enabled to move into the mainstream of American life. Some even made the step from "rags to riches" that the many had dreamed of. Left behind were those who could find no place in the larger community—chiefly individuals whose skin color relegated them to menial jobs, to fewer educational opportunities, and to restrictions on their choice of living quarters. With the aid of human service workers, well-intentioned individuals continued to organize and raise funds to help those of special concern to them and to provide facilities in disadvantaged neighborhoods. But change was slow in the human services in the community, just as in other fields. Private efforts could not begin to keep up with the need, and public funds were now committed for large welfare, housing, and health programs.

The Second World War brought new thousands to the cities and left them stranded when wartime industry and military service ended. Large housing developments, built to replace old unsanitary housing, concentrated many hopeless, angry, and needy people in impersonal structures that seemed more like prisons than homes. It was not surprising that the gang warfare that has always been a part of slum life now grew so that citizens of privileged neighborhoods became fearful. Vandalism, drug abuse, and welfare costs demanded the attention of the public and the help of many more human service workers than were then available.

Civil rights legislation, which reaffirmed the constitutional right of equal opportunity for all in education, employment, and choice of residence, alerted millions of people to the fact that many Americans had been denied these rights for hundreds of years. The legislation called for the appropriation of public funds to help the disadvantaged achieve what was their right. Extensive programs were planned and human service workers recruited in order to bring new opportunities to inner city residents and help them organize themselves so that they could successfully achieve their rightful status without the assistance of others. Toward these goals, many low-income residents were recruited to act as community human service workers. They not only carried out some of the tasks traditionally performed by such persons, but they also developed some new ways of bringing about change.

While, on the whole, these programs have reached many people, they have not accomplished the miracles hoped for. Those they were intended to help had, for generations, lived under conditions which reminded them hourly that they were different from their fellow citizens, that they were viewed by them as less worthy of the decencies and amenities of life, that no one cared what happened to them as long as they remained out of sight, and that because of the handicaps of color, poor education, and poverty, they were powerless to change their situation. It was not surprising that some of these people having ceased to expect help from anyone, including human service workers, rejected it when it was offered or used it to help them snatch what they believed would never be freely given.

Consequently, human service workers in the community today are exposed to severe and often painful pressures. They are in daily contact with people whose tremendous needs they want to help to meet. Yet their offers may be rejected. Or they may find that people are so grateful for help and able to use it so well that soon the intervention of a human service worker is no longer needed. But the directions in which people might go on their own may arouse new fears and distrust in the larger community which, in turn, may result in censure of the worker, withdrawal of needed funds, or both. Workers also face disappointment when individuals with potential for change and personal success and happiness are prevented by past circumstances of their lives from realizing this potential. And at all times, human service workers in the community have the added burden that their failures are public. Of course, all human service workers feel badly when they are unsuccessful in efforts to help others. In a hospital, for example, a nurse will deeply regret her inability to save a patient but she will not blame herself or be blamed by her colleagues for her failure when she has done all she can. On the other hand, if a neighborhood action group which a human service worker has helped to organize marches to city hall and demands better street lighting, the worker will likely be subject to reproach and even public criticism in the press for "inciting to violence." Nevertheless, or perhaps because today's community service worker must be able to work under difficult conditions, it is a growing field which offers an interesting challenge to persons with a diversity of background, experience, and training.

community organization: puerto rican action committee

It is more difficult to provide insights into actual community organization situations than it is to follow individual experiences because the former usually involves the interactions of many people, often at many meetings over a considerable span of time. When meetings are recorded verbatim, as on a tape recorder, the transcript is difficult to follow and time-consuming to read. Yet, a brief summary from the minutes does not give the flavor of the meeting or show the process of decision making. The report that follows avoids both these extremes, perhaps because it is the work of a skilled and perceptive journalist who succeeds in conveying the sense of the meeting of a group of neighborhood leaders and their subsequent action, and also an impression of the many threads of difference, compromise, and consensus by which such groups may move slowly but meaningfully forward. The role of the human service workers who helped these neighborhood people to carry out their tasks is only implied in the fact that the residents are able to organize themselves for action today, when only a few years ago this would have been impossible.

On a recent Thursday evening, we went down to Ninth street and Avenue C to attend a meeting of the Lower East Side Puerto Rican Action Committee, which had been formed to help calm the neighborhood following three consecutive evenings of rioting. Crowds of three or four hundred people, most of them young Puerto Ricans, had gathered each night and thrown bottles and debris at members of the Police Department's Tactical Patrol Force (T.P.F.), the mobile force that is brought into troubled areas as the need arises. Several store windows had been smashed in the disturbances, and about twenty people had been arrested. In the summer, life in the neighborhood of Avenue C is spent half out-of-doors, on the sidewalks and streets. That Thursday, several card tables had been set up outside the slum doors, and groups of teen-agers or whole families were sitting at them or on the steps of the houses or on car hoods, often listening to Spanish music on small radios that were turned up to their brassy peak volume. The paint on most houses in the neighborhood is peeling or else is caked with soot; the streets are littered with paper; and the stores, which are all very small, sell almost nothing that is new. (One storefront loan company offers "Loans in Three Hours.") Generally almost nothing is clean, shiny, or new. Even neon lights are rare, and at night most of the stores are conspicuously locked and barred with heavy gates or sheets of metal. There were two or three policemen on every block, standing around twirling their nightsticks—expressing by their casual bearing and slow movements, the kind of deliberate calmness and unprovocative unconcern that is now their usual manner in tense situations or at demonstrations. Each policeman carried either a green Army helmet or a shiny blue plastic riot helmet with a visor. The spic-and-span uniforms of these beefy young policemen and their well-polished patrol cars, which were easily the best-looking cars in the neighborhood, stood out in an imposing contrast to the cluttered and smudged appearance of the neighborhood and to the informal attire of the neighborhood people, for whom jackets and ties are strictly Sunday clothes.

The Puerto Rican Action Committee was scheduled to meet at six-thirty in the Hispanic American Veterans Association Hall

From "Action Committee" by Jonathan Schell, *The New Yorker*, August 10, 1968, pp. 20–23. Reprinted with the permission of The New Yorker Magazine, Inc., © 1968.

on Avenue C, between Ninth Street and Tenth Street. The hall, we found, was a tall-ceilinged, deep room taking up the whole second floor of a building that had a garage below. The floor was covered with linoleum, which was peeling in a few places, and a huge American flag hung on one wall, along with pictures of President Kennedy and President Franklin Roosevelt. About half a dozen tables were arranged in a square in the middle of the room. The sounds of voices, traffic, and radios came in from the street through open front windows. Before the meeting began, we talked with several of the men who were going to take part. All of them were Puerto Rican, and were connected with one neighborhood group or another, such as Mobilization for Youth, or the Community Action Program, which assists poor residents of the area to adapt to life in the city. We soon learned that they were just about unanimously agreed not only on the question of what caused the disturbances but also on the question of what should be done to prevent further outbreaks, in both the short run and the long run. We spoke to a Mr. Al Cardona, who told us, "It's the same story with all of these riots across the country. A small incident mushrooms into a full-scale civil disorder. The kids have no jobs, or lousy jobs. They're on the street all day—they've got a house but no home. There's no hope for the future, and they're bored. They're tired of the same old routine and tired of sharing one bottle of soda pop with three guys. And they want adventure. If I said, 'Let's go to Africa,' they'd say, 'Yeah, let's go,' just like that. They want excitement, and they've got nothing to lose, so when fifty cops show up and someone throws a few bottles, there's nothing to hold them back." Another man there for the meeting, Mr. Wally Rivera, told us that on the night of the first disturbance he had seen a young girl throw a bottle, and when he asked her why she had done it, she had answered, "I like to hear the sound of glass breaking on the sidewalk."

The members of the committee all agreed that the immediate cause of the outbreaks had been the sudden presence of large numbers of the Tactical Patrol Force in the neighborhood, and, as the first demand they made of the city, they had asked that their committee be consulted before the T.P.F. was sent in again. They also agreed that in the long run the community needed a whole series of improvements, which the press and television had already been talking about for some time, and which they themselves had been working for even longer—better education, better housing, more jobs, and less discrimination. The poor conditions and their remedies were so well known to this committee of social workers that they were hardly touched on in the meeting that followed.

But if the basic issues were only too familiar, the actual business of setting up a group and conducting effective meetings was new, and a heated debate grew up around the questions of who should be on the committee and who should become its leaders. Though the members were all known to each other, they had never got together as a group before. Most of the rivalries were shifting and ambiguous, and couldn't be readily defined—perhaps because the splits were not based on disagreements about issues—but quite a bit of the debate at the meeting centered on the question of whether the committee should join forces with a group of young men who called themselves the Real Great Society and had formed around a nucleus of ex-members of youth gangs which was supported by the Office of Economic Opportunity. The day after the rioting began, this group had held a demonstration in front of the local precinct headquarters, but later it had met with the police and had agreed to patrol the neighborhood, wearing armbands, in an effort to persuade people not to cause trouble. The Real Great Society had formulated a set of demands for jobs, parks, and housing, and was asking the Puerto Rican Action Committee to give these its support.

Before the meeting began, we spoke with Pedro Otero, the acting chairman of the Action Committee, about this issue, and he told us, "Our committee is the legitimate committee—it is the *empowered* committee. We are recognized by the Mayor. The other group must come to us. They say that we get money from our jobs with the city, but I have a grocery store and I can make thirty dollars a night. But I close it to work on this committee, so I lose thirty dollars a night. I go out in the streets to cool the place down, and I take risks. I've lived here for thirty years, and I know everyone here personally. I am a man of the people. But there are some who don't care about anything, who have no commitment, and I don't care to lead them. I don't care about them."

We asked Mr. Rivera what he thought of the people who made up the committee, and he said, "I don't think some of them are really leaders. I mean, who do they lead? Who knows about them? Some of them just want to get power for themselves. They're doing it to make a political position for themselves. I don't care about being a leader myself. I just want to do my job in obscurity. People come to me and say, 'Wally, help me. My husband's in jail,' or 'I can't get any welfare.' That's all." Mr.

Rivera's position of criticizing "some people" as false leaders but disclaiming any ambition to be a leader himself was a popular one that evening. When the people there spoke to us, or to each other, they often started out by saying something like "now, I don't pretend to be any kind of leader, but. . . ."

Just as the meeting was about to begin, five tough-looking members of the Real Great Society walked in. After brief, uneasy consultations, they were allowed to sit, all together, at one end of the group of tables. Most of them appeared to be in their early twenties. Their leader was wearing dark glasses and had a slightly drooping mustache. They all looked about them warily, with looks that seemed to express a kind of prideful scorn of what they saw. Mr. Otero opened the meeting by reading the agenda, which consisted, first, of decisions to be made about a conference that was to be held with Manny Diaz, Deputy Commissioner of the Manpower and Career Development Agency, and, second, of the question of what means to employ to keep the peace in the neighborhood that night, but, as it turned out, the agenda was forgotten. The first speaker Mr. Otero recognized was Pablo Garcia, who had seemed unhappy when the group of young men from the Real Great Society came in. "Now, look," Garcia said. "We're all people of good faith here together, trying to do the best thing for the community, and we don't want to have any hypocritical promises from any of you. We don't want you here if you're going to talk nice with us but then go out and throw bottles at the cops on the street." Several members of the younger group protested, and Mr. Garcia, apparently interpreting their restlessness as a sign that they were about to leave, said "Nobody leaves yet!" and then got up and went over and closed the door that led downstairs. The five young men jumped up as one man from their chairs and made for the door. "Nobody closes the door on us!" one shouted. Several other men, who were nearer the door, jumped up, too, and, making it to the door before the Real Great Society people, opened it, assured them that it would remain open, and persuaded them to sit down again.

Up to this point, the meeting had been conducted half in English and half in Spanish. Now Mr. Garcia moved that the official language of the meeting be Spanish, and the motion was carried. Mr. Otero then told the young group that if they wanted to work with the Action committee, they would have to give their names to the secretary.

The young man in sunglasses answered, in English, "We don't

have to tell our names. What do you want to know our names for? Why don't you tell your names?"

Several people tried to speak at once, and Mr. Otero banged the table with his hand for order. "If you're going to come here and work with the committee, you have to accept the committee's authority," he said heatedly, in Spanish. "We will work only on this basis."

The young man in sunglasses answered loudly, still speaking English, "The reason these cats won't tell their names is that they're getting a big fat *salary* from politicians and aren't doing one damn thing for the people."

Mr. Rivera broke in to recommend that *everyone* give his name, and everyone then did.

Afterward, several people again started talking at once, and Mr. Otero banged his hand on the table and said, "Order! Order! I recognize Rocky." He indicated a handsome man with a pencil mustache.

Rocky stood up and made an impassioned criticism of "some of the established leaders," which he wound up by saying, "I'm no intellectual. I've had only a second-grade education and I used to be a boxer, and I don't use any Sunday-school words. I'm sick of so-called leaders who don't do a damn thing. There are some people who could do something if they were given a chance. But now every one cuts each other's throat, and when a proposal to give jobs is made, they staff it with their own friends. The people are tired of this. We people in the community want new faces!"

Other speakers also expressed the opinion that new leaders were needed, although they were quick to add that they themselves had no aspirations to become leaders.

After fifteen minutes of this general airing of views, the young man in sunglasses, whose name had turned out to be Artie Santiago, angrily cut in to say, in English, "O.K., look, All I hear is a lot of talk—"

"In Spanish! In Spanish!" several voices cried out.

Mr. Santiago started again, softly in Spanish, and a look of panic flickered in his eyes. Then, loud and angry again, he said, in English, "Look. I'm gonna talk now, and you're going to *listen,* and I'm going to talk English because I'm third-generation and my Spanish is *terrible.* It stinks!"

"We agreed on Spanish. That's the rule," Mr. Otero said, but others called out "We'll make an exception!" and Mr. Otero relented.

"O.K. Now all I hear is talk," Mr. Santiago continued. "Crap! It's all crap! Now, you get *this,* man. We're the *youth,* we represent the majority of the youth, and we've got our *own* committee! How do you like that? I'm just showing you how big the *crap* is! You're going to give us a chance to *learn* and *lead* and do our thing." Then he criticized the leaders of the committee, and added that he himself was not a leader but merely a spokesman for his committee. "I'm nothing to the kids," he said. He then pulled out a sheet of paper and went on, "We've got some *demands,* and we don't expect you'll support them, but here they are." He read a list of twenty-one demands to be made of the city. The demands—for five thousand more jobs for New York Puerto Ricans, a Puerto Rican high-school principal, an I.B.M. program for Puerto Ricans, lights in parks at night, garbage cans on street corners, and a program of Puerto Rican history to be taught in summer schools, among other things—constituted a full catalogue of those improvements that people concerned about the slums had always asked for and although they were very ambitious, not one proved unacceptable to the older group of men. The group of five then asked whether the committee would support the demands. Mr. Otero said that if the committee did, then the Real Great Society would have to submit to the authority of the committee.

Next, a man delivered a talk in which he said that he had fought in the Korean War and was now employed as a truck driver at a hundred and fifty dollars a week. The young people, he said, were not the only ones with a right to live. In the riots, people near him had thrown bottles, and then *he* had had to face the detectives and police. There were more short speeches, and finally someone called out "Let's vote!"

The issue of whether the younger group was to get the support of the older group only if it submitted to the older group's authority was not brought up again, and the vote went unanimously in favor of supporting the younger group's demands. When this happened, the younger group jumped up, its members laughing and talking and shaking hands with each other. Mr. Otero pounded the table for order.

Once calm had been restored, Mr. Santiago said he wanted to make one point clear. "What I mean is, what the youth want is to have a *majority* of the seats on the committee—we're demanding a majority," he said. It was the first time this point had been brought up, but just as he spoke, several of the men at the other end of the room began to argue with each other about something else, and they paid attention only to Mr. Santiago's

next remark, which was that he had to confer with his own committee before he made any binding agreements to anything.

Generally, throughout the meeting, there seemed to be a willingness to preserve a spirit of agreement by stretching and pulling parliamentary procedure in a way that kept the thorniest
issues from coming to the fore and allowed the subject to change
before any single issue could really inflame the participants.

At about nine-thirty, we accompanied Wally Rivera over to
the Ninth Precinct Headquarters, on Fifth Street. He was one of
two representatives of the Action Committee who would be
posted at the station house to serve as liaison men between the
committee and the police in case there was trouble. On the way
over, he explained to us that the police had agreed to let the
committee try to calm down any disturbances before the T.P.F.
was sent in. At the station house, we talked with the precinct
chief, Deputy Inspector Joseph Fink—the man who had distrib-
uted armbands to the Real Great Society. He expressed satisfaction with the calm prevailing that night, and he told us that
he was working with the Puerto Rican Action Committee and
was glad to find that the community leaders shared his interest
in preventing riots. Not all the policemen shared Inspector
Fink's interpretation of the situation, however. One lieutenant
we talked with lumped the rioters and the committee that was
trying to stop the riots in one hostile group. For him, the fact
that both the rioters and the committee opposed the presence of
the T.P.F. in the community was enough to prove that the two
groups were one.

A little later, Mr. Rivera remarked to Inspector Fink, "I'm here
according to the agreement with the Action Committee about
not sending the T.P.F. into the community without getting the
agreement of the Action Committee."

"What?" Inspector Fink exclaimed. "We didn't agree to that."

For a moment, it seemed that the whole arrangement might
fall apart. It seemed that the Action Committee might have convinced itself that the agreement had given it more power than it
really had, and also that Inspector Fink might have gone back
to a tougher line. But then, perhaps sensing the danger of a split,
Inspector Fink added, "Of course, we'll let you know in advance
if we do anything."

"Right. You'll consult with us before you do anything," said
Mr. Rivera.

Both men seemed relieved. To us it appeared that in this encounter, as in the one between the Action Committee and the
Real Great Society people, when precise agreements could not

be worked out between groups, each side tended to give the other side's position an interpretation that was charitable almost to the point of distortion. The Action Committee had apparently allowed itself to believe that the police would not move without its permission— an interpretation that gave it considerable authority in its own community—and the police had apparently come to think that the committee would be satisfied merely with advance notice. It almost seemed that, in this atmosphere of first gropings toward a unified Puerto Rican community organization and toward better communication with the police, the will to agree had taken precedence over the substance of the agreements, and in this spirit a makeshift peace had been effected.

It would be deceptive to assume that human service workers in every community action program achieved the degree of success that is reflected above. On the contrary, many human service workers have found that the demands of large public bureaucracies tend to impose restrictions and requirements on local programs that have actually prevented them from serving those in the community who most needed help—the individuals and groups that did not participate in programs organized for them.

residential youth center: boys and staff

The following account is taken from a book about a project that grew out of the disappointment of some members of the staff with a large community action program in an Eastern city. It was written in the first person by the organizer of the Residential Youth Center and its first director, who held a doctoral degree in psychology and was a professor at a famous university.

As a program, the RYC was to house 20 youngsters and work with 20 families at any one time. Over the year, the program was to serve 50 residents and families. Each resident was assigned a worker. It was the worker's responsibility, using whatever means and techniques at his disposal, to get to know his

Reprinted from *Build Me a Mountain* by Ira Goldenberg (Cambridge, Mass.: M.I.T. Press) with the permission of the publisher. Copyright © 1971 by Massachusetts Institute of Technology.

youngster and family "like a book" and to use himself as a thera-
peutic lever in their lives.* The worker's "job" was to gain ac-
cess into and earn the trust and respect of people who had come
to fear, distrust, and, in some cases, despise "change agents"
(e.g., welfare workers, social workers, school and law enforce-
ment personnel) of one sort or another. The formal goals of the
program were simple and clear enough: (1) to help the youngster
and his family become employed or enter employment opportunity programs that they wanted; (2) to help them deal with
some of the barriers or problems (psychological, social, or other)
that stood between them and a life that was more fulfilling and
satisfying; and (3) to make it possible within a relatively short
period of time (6 months) for the youngster either to return home
or to establish himself in his own apartment. It is important to
point out and to repeat that with the exception of preparing a
youngster to leave the RYC physically, the aims of the program
with respect to its clients were essentially no different from its
goals for its own staff. In both cases, creating the conditions for
individual and collective growth were the primary purposes behind the development of the setting.

On a theoretical basis it was hoped that during the day the
residents would be out of the RYC (hopefully) attending work.
The worker could use this time to visit his youngster's work site,
but it was also a time to work with the boy's family. During the
evenings and on weekends the RYC was to be used for special
programs. These programs were open to all residents (eventually,
to the entire community) and their families. . . .

At no time was the program to be allowed to become or to
resemble an institution: there were no visiting hours, parents
were encouraged to come at any time of the day or night, the
residents paid rent, and the boys were free to go home anytime
they wanted. The program, both formally and informally, was to
consist of a house in which people—not "patients" or "inmates"
—could work and live with one another, could grow and begin
to perceive themselves as no longer powerless to alter and influence their lives, and perhaps more than anything else, could
begin to make sense out of the paradoxical and oftentimes contradictory world we all share. . . .

. . . Staffing the RYC had more to do with getting certain kinds

---

* "Working with" the boys at the RYC was to come to mean being with them,
fighting with them, counseling them, and experiencing and sharing their successes and failures on a 24-hour basis. The same was true of working with their
families. In both cases it meant becoming involved with them in ways and
through paths that most "helping" people would not or could not travel.

of *people* than with getting certain kinds of *credentials*. Consequently, the basic criteria for selecting staff had to do with (1) the amount of observable or inferable commitment and involvement that a candidate indicated toward the work, and (2) the amount and kind of experience the individual had in working with members of the target population. . . .

The selection of staff for the RYC was direct. No tests of any kind (e.g., aptitude, value profile, or intelligence tests) were given to any of the candidates. Anyone wanting to work at the RYC was interviewed by the program's Director and Deputy Director. The interview consisted of explaining the program to the candidate, eliciting his reactions, and discussing the problems and uncertainties of the program with him. . . . *First, we wanted people who were dissatisfied—and who were willing to voice their dissatisfaction—with the limitations and restrictions imposed upon them by their current role in the community action program. . . . And second, we wanted people who not only were committed and dedicated to working with the poor but were also both willing to experiment with a variety of different helping techniques (knowing well that none of them offered any guarantee of being effective) and ready to face the inevitable anxiety that such a venture would produce. . . .*

the original ryc staff

Nine people made up the original staff of the RYC. Eight were males, and one (the secretary) was a female; five were white, four were black. By and large the staff could properly be called indigenous to the inner-city community; in the cases in which the people were not indigenous by birth they were certainly "indigenous" in terms of past experience, length of inner-city residence, or socioeconomic background. . . . Of the original nine staff members, only one had a professional degree. Most of the staff had high school diplomas, one had had a year of business college, and one was a high school dropout. . . .

the original clients

The RYC was funded to work with those youngsters (boys between the ages of 16 and 21 who were both out of school and out of work) and families that fell into the so-called hard-core classification. They were, in point of fact, people on whom just about everyone had given up; and by "everyone" we mean both the traditional agencies (i.e., the schools, the Welfare Department, and the mental health professions) and the not-so-traditional agency, the community action program itself. . . .

Of the first 20 youngsters to enter the program, 12 were Negro and 8 were white. Although their ages ranged from 16 to 20, the average age was 17.4 years. Seventy percent of the residents had been arrested one or more times prior to their entry into the RYC program. . . . Only 3 of the boys had never spent any time in an institution of one sort or another; 85 percent of the youngsters had been incarcerated in jail, a reformatory, an institution for the mentally retarded, a center for emotionally disturbed and homeless children, or a state facility for the mentally ill. . . .

[On the day that the RYC opened, the boys and staff spent exhausting hours moving in.]

day two: 9/17/66

. . . When I came in, I found Scotty [deputy director] slumped over a cup of coffee and looking down at the table in front of him as if it held some strange attraction that only he could appreciate. When he looked up at me I wasn't sure for a second whether he was going to smile, cry, or belt me in the mouth. . . . He just kind of stared right past me so I figured it was safe to sit down. After ignoring me for about three minutes, he told me what had happened.

Seems that the kids decided that the RYC would make a good 24-hour playground, and they devoted their first evening in the house to testing that assumption. They were up and down the stairs almost all night, laughing, screaming, fighting, playing their record players at ear-shattering volume, and generally trying as hard as possible to topple the RYC through their frenzied activity. Scotty and Lance were like firemen trying to deal with a dozen different fires at the same time. No sooner would it seem as if they had controlled one fire when another would break out somewhere else in the house. . . .

The kids pulled one other thing that we really didn't expect. It seems that the roof here at the RYC holds some particularly great fascination for a lot of the boys. By climbing out of their windows and straddling the ledge they were able to go sit on the roof and stare into the windows of some of the people who live across the way. The fascination is clear: there's a good-looking girl living across the way and the kids were hoping to get a look at her while she was undressing for bed. Tonight, at least, their quest was in vain. Still, this climbing on the roof is going to be a problem. Not only could it lead to trouble with the neighbors (the kind of trouble we sure as hell don't need), but it's also dangerous, and one false step by a kid up on the roof could be disastrous.

Since the kids were up virtually the whole night, very few of them were able to get up and get out of the house in time to make it to their jobs. . . .

day three: 9/18/66

It was murder, just plain murder. No matter how much I try I can't find anything even remotely amusing (not to mention hopeful) to write about what went on last night.

The kids decided to stay up all night, and they all damn near did it. From the time most of the staff left for the night until early this morning (around 5:45 a.m.), the RYC was the scene of some of the wildest and, at times, some of the most frightening things I've ever seen. It was like some bizarre circus concocted by a demented ringmaster.

To begin with, as has become almost expected, the kids were all in the house by midnight after threatening to stay away all night. . . . They seemed to dig into their bag of tricks and continually came up with something new, something just a little more bizarre, a little more infuriating, a little more dangerous than whatever had gone on before. For example, Cliff swinging from the light fixtures at 2:00 a.m., . . . back and forth, a diabolical gleam all over his face as he threw light bulbs against the living-room walls, laughing as each bulb went crashing into the wall, shattering all those around him with a thin stream of pouring glass. For example, Wayne sitting in the dining room, staring at a piece of buttered bread in his hand, and finally throwing it against the wall to the accompaniment of his own blood-curdling shriek. And later, Wayne again, sitting on the couch, his head bent low to the ground, spitting all over his bare toes and giggling some far away giggle. For example, Shorty, Monty, and Bucky doing a high-wire act on the roof at 3:00 in the morning. . . .

day four: 9/19/66

It doesn't look as if the end is in sight. Last night was a repetition of what has now been going on ever since we opened the Center. Butch was on duty to help Lance, Vito, and Clark. I just can't stand going into details so I'll just list what went on.

1. A sink was torn out of the bathroom wall on the third floor. Most of the staff believe it was Wayne's doing but, naturally, nobody's talking.

2. Somebody broke Marty's mirror.

3. During the night Wayne was taken to the hospital with a cut over his eye.

4. We suspect that Tim has been sniffing glue.

5. Someone has been urinating in Ev and Marty's room and defecating in their closet.

6. The kids stayed up just about the whole night again. . . .

Today's staff meeting did result in a few decisions that might be helpful. Everyone felt that the live-ins were under even greater pressure than the rest of the staff. Consequently, in addition to the staff member who joins the live-ins on duty each night, it was decided that the rest of us would be considered on duty regardless of the time of day or night. Thus, for example, if Cliff is acting up (as he always seems to be), and if the people on staff do not feel that they can handle him, Jack (his worker) would be called into the situation regardless of whether or not he was "officially" on duty. I use Cliff as an example simply because he seems to be the kid who presents everyone (except Jack) with the greatest number of problems. Although Jack thought the decision was a good one, he made it clear that in the long run he expected each and everyone of us to learn to be able to handle Cliff as well as he can. He felt that if we began to rely solely on a kid's worker to handle a particular kid, we would be creating a situation in which the kids were both denied the opportunity of interacting with a variety of different people and placed in the position of viewing themselves as dependent on a particular person for help. We all agreed with Jack's cautioning remarks, but I for one, perhaps because I find Cliff such a frightening and unpredictable kid, felt relieved to know that Jack was now "officially" on duty all the time. . . .

day five: 9/20/66

Another night of the same; maybe a little tougher, maybe not. . . .

Last night the kids decided to give the pool table a real workout. About six of them shot pool from about 7:00 p.m. until the wee hours of the morning. The pool table is down in the basement, but the shouting could be heard all over the house. In addition to playing pool, however, some of the guys (mostly Tim, Leland, and Bucky) decided that the pipes in the basement could be used as chinning bars and they almost ripped the pipes down from the basement ceiling. Also, since we do not as yet have any chalk for the pool sticks, they began using the ceiling of the basement (the plaster) as their source of chalk. The result was that they almost punched a dozen holes in the ceiling. By the time we finally stopped them, the basement floor was covered with pieces of fallen plaster. . . .

day six: 9/21/66

This is really quite a staff. You walk in here in 1:00 in the morning and there's Jack shooting pool with the kids in the basement. I say to Jack, "Hey man, what're you doing down here? You're not on tonight, why don't you go home and look in on the wife?" Jack looks up, smiles, and says, "Oh, I just felt like shooting a game of pool with Wayne and Cliff so I came down." Or get ready to leave about 10:00 p.m., and as you're walking out of the RYC you see Butch and Chip drive up. You go over and ask them what they're doing around the Center at this time of night and they say, ever so nonchalantly: "Well, we were just driving by and we figured we'd stop in for a few minutes." And you walk away knowing that Butch and Chip are there for the night even though they're supposed to be off duty. That's the way this staff is and it's probably one of the few things that keeps us going. I don't know how to explain it, and maybe I shouldn't even try. All I know is that while we've never talked about it, it seems as though everyone has made the same silent decision: "This is my place and it's more than a place to work. It's the place I want to be, the place I helped to build, and the place I'm going to make damn sure 'makes it.'" What more can I say? I don't know what the future's going to be like—don't even know if we have a future—but right now I look around me and feel that come what may, this is one very special group of people I work with. . . .

day eight: 9/23/66

. . . While the situation as a whole was not noticeably different than it's been ever since we opened the place (it seems as if it's been about ten years since we first opened up), Jack, who was on duty, reported his feeling that there had been a slight change in the quality of the nighttime chaos. Last night he got the distinct impression that the kids were beginning to tire, both physically and emotionally, of their nightly commitment to "exuberance" (Jack broke up when he used the word). It's his feeling that the kids are just about ready, indeed almost begging, for us to say "that's it" and put an end to the madness. Almost everyone at the staff meeting agreed with his analysis, but we decided to let the kids have at least one more crack at instituting their own curfew through the House Council before we stepped into the situation. . . .

day nine: 9/24/66

Well, today was C-Day (Curfew Day). Last night was no different from every other night (i.e., the kids were up most of the night and didn't get to bed until the wee hours of the morning), and so today we got them all together to go over the situation and to let them know of our decision to impose a curfew. I think most of the kids knew what was coming, and although I may be kidding myself, I really believe that some of the kids were really relieved when it finally happened. . . .

The meeting began with Scotty reviewing the evening action in all its "splendor." Scotty has a way of describing things in such a manner that one's immediate impression is that while he may be relating "awful things" he is *not* condemning or pointing the finger at certain individuals to the exclusion of others (including the staff). At any rate, Scotty went over what's been happening, reviewed our initial hopes that the kids themselves would have been able to control the situation, and concluded by summarizing the staff's reasons for feeling that the time had come for us to take the initial step toward the imposition of additional structure.

When he finished, Scotty, still not having mentioned the specific curfew decided upon by the staff, threw the question out on the floor and asked for the kids' comments and reactions. Despite some grumbling and squirming, the kids, I think somewhat taken aback by the apparent lack of anger in the way Scotty presented the problem, remained relatively quiet.

At this point the rest of us (the staff) joined the conversation. Each of us, in turn, recounted the effects of the evening chaos on "our own" kids. Jack, for example, was able to review the problems that lack of sleep had created for Cliff, Wayne, and Bucky. Butch followed with his own problems regarding Tim, Ev, and Robbie. I, and then Lance and Chip reviewed what had been happening to Shorty, Heinz, and Curt. And so on. In a way I guess we were confronting the kids, en masse, with the "catalog of horrors" that the nighttime chaos has been causing for ourselves, the kids, and the RYC in general. Most of us were pretty graphic in our descriptions, and we made no attempt to avoid communicating our own feelings about the situation and how it has been affecting us as individuals. . . .

By this time the kids had sunk deep down into their chairs

and were just waiting to hear what the curfew would be. I then told them that the staff had decided that during the work week (Sunday night through Thursday night) they had to be in bed by 1:00 a.m., and that on Friday and Saturday nights the curfew was 3:00 a.m. . . . The kids were floored. They were expecting a curfew, maybe something like 9:00 or 10:00 p.m., that was not only restricting but also repressive, and here we were saying that we had no intention of punishing the kids but only wanted to provide a curfew that would enable them to get enough sleep so that they could make it to work in the morning.* The response was unbelievable. No response at all. They kind of looked at each other, at the staff, and again at each other. I think what happened was that they were really thrown off balance. I think they were prepared to fight the staff's "expected" decision but were now in the uncomfortable position of having much of the fight (i.e., the anticipated nature of the "punishment") begin to look unreasonable by virtue of the curfew we were now imposing. How the hell can you really get mad about something that makes sense, isn't "way out," and isn't imposed in an atmosphere of vengeance?

Anyway, after a few minutes, the kids recovered their cool and quickly discovered that a 1:00 a.m. curfew would mean that they couldn't finish watching the Late Show on TV. (the late movie is not generally over until about 1:20 a.m.). With the issue of being able to watch the completion of the Late Show their new "cause" (and a face-saving one at that), the kids quickly banded together to present the staff with a united front for purposes of bargaining. From the point of view of the staff, the kids were presenting an eminently reasonable request, and after only a few minutes of negotiation it was decided that the 1:00 a.m. curfew would "really" mean the time that the Late Show was over, but that if there was any abuse of this "concession," the curfew would revert back to 1:00 a.m., regardless of what was happening on the boob tube. . . .

day ten: 9/25/66

. . . Last night we had our first quiet night at the RYC. Everyone was in the house by 11:00 p.m. and . . . all the kids were either in bed or asleep by 1:30 a.m. A few of the kids . . . didn't even wait

---

* Some weeks later, when the House Council had become established and was functioning on a regular basis, the residents confirmed what much of the research on adolescents has shown; namely, that teenagers, when given the opportunity of establishing their own rules and regulations, are usually more severe on themselves than are adults. They *reduced* the staff's workweek curfew for themselves from 1:00 a.m. to midnight.

until curfew time before going to bed. . . .Most of the guys did stay up to watch the Late Show but dutifully went up to bed as soon as it was over and Lance had turned off the TV set. A couple of kids . . . looked as if they were going to "test" Lance and said that they weren't going to go to sleep, but when they found no support from the other kids, they too dragged their tails up to bed. . . .

[Some days later]

The evening of the next scheduled dance started quietly enough. The residents, their dates, and the invited guests showed up as usual. In a little while the sounds of the "Bugaloo," the "Watusi," and the "Skate," filled the air as the youngsters danced, drank (soft drinks, of course), and enjoyed themselves. Around 11:00 p.m. a number of kids from the surrounding neighborhoods appeared on the scene and wanted to get into the house and join the party. Some of the residents and staff met them at the porch and told them that they could not come in. They also tried to explain to them the reasons why it was impossible (it was actually against the law) for any more people to congregate in the house. Some of the boys in the group outside the RYC began talking of "crashing" the party. Things became tense and the youngsters inside the house began making preparations for the expected assault. The kids outside started milling around.

At this point two RYC staff members, one white and the other black, came out to the porch to try to talk to the group, a group now becoming angrier and more restless with each passing second. Most of the youngsters standing outside the RYC were black, and the black staff member began to talk with them. In a short while the kids began taunting the white staff member, cursing him, and calling him "Whitey" and "Honky." Suddenly the white staff member broke from the porch, waded into the group, and the melee was on. Other staff members came out of the house, pulled the white staff member out of the crowd, and dragged him back through the doorway and into the Center. There was a good deal of pushing and punching going on, and the police finally were summoned. By the time they arrived most of the fighting was over. The remaining youngsters ran away as the squad cars approached. The party was over—for everyone.

As soon as the police had gone and the house was "bedded down" for the night, those of us who were still there went into the office to talk about what happened. Although the discussion started out with the goal of "formulating policy" with respect to future dances, it soon became clear that what was really troubling the group and what we really had to talk about were the feelings touched off by what we all agreed was clearly a racial incident. . . .

BUTCH:* Well, as we talked about it, about what happened and everything, there were a couple of things that struck me funny. I think I have learned something out of it. It was kind of worth the bruises that I got out of it. I really didn't honestly think there was as much hatred between black and white as there is in New Haven. This past night was maybe the first time I honestly knew what it meant to be colored. I was white and they were crucifying me for it. All I heard was, "Whitey, over there, you keep your goddamned mouth shut. You don't say a word." This I think really started the whole incident because after a while, my tem-per started burning to a point where I don't know whether I wanted to turn around and scream, "Why, you crazy bastard, what are you trying to prove? I am working with you, you know. I am not against you. I am with you."

I honestly didn't think they saw this. I am not denying that I have got some racial prejudice, because I have. But I do feel that I took too much for granted; that, you know, just because we are open-minded and can talk and can socialize and think nothing of going to restaurants and think nothing of going out together, and think nothing of kidding around, that more or less everybody was supposed to feel the same way. I just found out that isn't so.

KELLY: It kind of sounds like two things. First of all, you blew your cool. The second thing was that you suddenly began to see the world, I think, through the eyes of the Negro kids, except you were on the other side this time.

BUTCH: I used to run into a lot of cases where a bunch of kids would be trying to bust into a place or start a rumpus, but I knew them by sight, and we could kid around. I could walk in and say, "Hey, baby, cool it." And one of the guys was sure to say, "Take it easy, he's all right. He's from CPI [Community Progress, Inc.] I know him."

What really got me this time was out of the clear blue sky, all of a sudden, this "Whitey" bit comes in, and I couldn't figure it out for the love of me. After a while, after I heard it ten or fifteen times, I could have cared less about nonviolence or anything. The same way, the other thing that scared the living shit out of me, when I got into the fight, I didn't have any fear of being cut or

* For purposes of identification, we should point out that Kelly, Butch, Sterns, Lance, and Chip are white; Scotty, Jack, Clark, Silver, and Jean are black.

anything like that or getting belted. I just had the greatest god-damned urge to kill somebody up there.

JACK: Was this before you were hit or after when you got this opinion of wanting to kill somebody?

BUTCH: During it. I think it started right after the first blow was swung.

JACK: That's what I mean, before or after you were hit?

BUTCH: I think it started right there. Suddenly I had this kid up against the wall. All I could think of is that I wanted to really kill the kid. I think if I would have carried a gun I would have killed the kid.

STERNS: Were you thinking in racial terms about the kid then?

BUTCH: I can't honestly say. I don't know. I had such an urge. I have been born and raised in gang fights. I have been born and raised in barroom fights in the service, but I rarely ever had that urge like I did last night to kill. If anything, I would have to say it was a racial overtone. . . .

JACK: What you were saying before, if you can remember, during the time of the incident, I was doing most of the talking. Every once in a while you would come in and comment. When the kids started with the "Whitey" bit you started talking a lot more. Then I knew the real trouble was coming. They accepted me but they weren't going to accept nothing you said. All it could do was get things more excited. They didn't want to hear you or listen to you.

BUTCH: But if colored kids aren't going to listen to me, to a white guy, how am I going to work with them as an RYC worker? Even though the fight was not with RYC kids, but with kids from the outside, how can I have a bona fide relationship with a colored kid if there is always that under-hidden hatred for a white versus colored.

The same way, now, maybe I will be saying, "Why that black bastard, I can't stand his guts." Do I now go and find another way of working with colored kids? . . .

KELLY: Chip, you were a cop for a lot of years and you had to be involved in a lot of very tense situations involving black people and white people. What happened there? What were your feelings?

CHIP: I was neutral. I just tried to treat them all the same. I didn't care whether they were black or white. If they were doing something they weren't supposed to be doing they got treated the same way. I was too busy to think.

JACK: What Kelly is saying, during the course of the period when you were a police officer, you arrested Negro kids and arrested white kids, or both at the same time. Weren't there times when, say, you arrested a new Negro kid when he gave you a tongue-lashing as the white person arresting him?

CHIP: You get that all the time. "You're only arresting me because I'm colored." You get this bit every time you arrest one of them. . . .

. . . I've been called a few choice names and you're right. You know, I didn't feel good about it. . . .

. . . I knew how the people felt.

KELLY: How did you know how these people felt?

CHIP: Because you hear it all the time. We were practically living with them. When you're working up on Dixwell Avenue, you're living with them.

KELLY: What do you think the Negro people feel?

CHIP: They hated—not because I was white, but because I was a cop. They hated you just because you're a cop. Whether it's white or Negro you have got that uniform on and that's it. They don't like you. . . .

SCOTTY: Can I speak as a Negro? (laughter) I'd like to say a few things that I felt and that I've seen, you know, through my life and growing up. Right from the beginning a Negro has to fight for survival. Growing up you find that because you're a Negro there are quite a few doors closed to you. Like coming up through high school, maybe you had a counselor where you knew you were doing better than a white kid, but your counselor would gear you to just get you through school and maybe go through a trade school, while the white kid was geared to college.

Coming up, you go to an integrated school and get to make friends with some white and colored. Me as an individual, I always rated a person depending on how they treated me. Whether they were black or white didn't make any difference.

JACK: After you grew up—

SCOTTY: Let me finish. But you find you lose a lot of these feelings after junior high school and high school. You know, you can go to their homes and this and that. But then I think what turns it back is the minute you graduate from high school all this changes.

As a kid, I can go into his house and play with him, play with his little sister or something like that, but now I'm an adult, you know, and I'm out of high school. All of a sudden the white friends that I went to school with, some of them stopped speaking to me. Some of them didn't want to associate with me.

I even know people that I graduate with, I can't get as much as a "hello" from them. So you begin saying, "Well, maybe a lot that I learned that my parents told me is true about white people." When persons turn around and you find out they are not what you think they are, this makes you twice as hard, you know, toward this race. When I found out some of the things they were doing and saying behind my back, this made me bring back all my feelings that I was taught as a kid. You know, they are reinforced twice as hard. This was my feeling, you can't trust them. Italians, you can't trust them. They befriend you and talk behind your back, stab you in the back. This is what I have experienced. I mean I used to go into this kid's house and sit down and eat with him every day. As a friend I said to him, "Mike, if you had a sister—me and you are just like brothers now—if you had a sister and I wanted to marry her, how would you feel? He came out and told me, he said, "I wouldn't want it. I want to be your friend. I'll tell you the truth. I'd hate your guts," he said.

Different things like that makes you change. . . .

It was mentioned earlier that one way in which human service workers traditionally have worked in the community is to help humanitarian individuals in the middle and upper classes organize and become active on behalf of others. The civil rights demonstrations of the early sixties gave rise to many such organizations under many different kinds of leadership. They attracted as workers young people who had only recently become aware of the deepseated and tragic problems facing minority groups. Many of these young people were serious and devoted—some even to death—to the causes they worked for and developed a great deal of skill in their chosen jobs. Others, attracted perhaps by the glamour and popular appeal and visibility given to the movements, plunged into them in the role of human service worker-leaders with very little real understanding of the situation or of themselves. Such a one was Harry Conrad who is next described in a novel about a neighborhood so terribly deteriorated and so long without hope that the people who live there, most of them prostitutes, pimps, drug users and petty criminals, would be unlikely to respond to the efforts of much more skilled and serious workers than he.

street organizing:
harry conrad

Conrad, a young man from a comfortable white middle-class background, has recently graduated from college, "discovered" the Negro problem, and gone to work for an organization which is seeking
to help black people win their rights through picketing those busi-
nesses that are unfair to them in employment practices. He comes
to Howard Street to organize such a demonstration against a local
store and meets Jackie Brown, a life-long resident, not much older
than himself in years but far more bitterly experienced. Once an
ambitious boy, Jackie had received an athletic scholarship and left
the neighborhood for college and the beginning of a new life. But
there had been no one at the college to help him to make the many
difficult adjustments demanded of him by the strange and often
hostile new setting and he had been unable to do so alone. He had
returned to Howard Street and a miserable, self-destructive life of
drinking, petty stealing and the companionship of people he hated
and dared not leave. The conversation below takes place in a bar
which Jackie has chosen, hoping to cadge some drinks and cigarettes. In answer to Conrad's inquiries he says:

"You came to the wrong place, mister. Ain't nobody around here
interested in demonstratin' for nothin' except more wine, more
dope, and more johns for the whores." . . .
Conrad ordered two more drinks, then said, "It certainly looks
that way, Jackie." His manner was almost apologetic. "However,
once the people in this section realize that what we're trying to
accomplish is in their own best interests, I'm sure that we'll meet
with much better success." He was a tall man, with wavy black
hair and deep-set blue eyes. . . .
Jackie said, "I'll let you in on a secret, buddy: it's gonna take
another hundred years for the people around here to even realize
what the hell you talkin' about, much less do somethin' about it.
I'm a goddamn tramp, right? But I got this way by tryin' to do just
what you're doin' now. You can't talk that freedom stuff to these
hip people, man. They don't wanna hear—mainly because they
don't wanna change their way of life. Too much effort. Workin'

From *Howard Street* by Nathan C. Heard (New York: Dial Press), pp. 149–155, 159–
165. Copyright © 1968 by Nathan C. Heard. Reprinted with the permission of the
publisher and Paul R. Reynolds, Inc., New York.

ain't no attraction for them. If you ain't got no money to give away then you might as well forgit it."

Harry looked at Jackie's bloated face with pity and mild repugnance—at the cracked and shriveled lips, the week-old beard, the lines of caked dirt shooting across Jackie's forehead. This was only Harry's second time in the field, actually working on his own among the city's poverty-stricken people, and neither his experience nor his CR training at headquarters had prepared him for the Jackie Browns, or for the squalor, violence, and apathy that he'd found on Howard Street. The blacks he'd known in school and at headquarters were nothing like these people. . . .

But, as Jackie Brown had observed, he was getting nowhere fast on Howard Street. It would have been much easier to have people from the CR headquarters and its affiliates demonstrate, but CR leaders thought it best that the task force be the people directly involved in the neighborhood. Then none of the stores could claim that it was only "outside agitators" who were responsible for the "trouble." Hope drawn from the CR people had been the only thing to sustain him since he had taken an active part in their movement. He needed now more than ever to cling to that hope.

Meanwhile, Jackie, with the whiskey in him, was feeling pretty good. His heart beat fast, because he wasn't used to good whiskey anymore, but his high was much warmer and fuller than the one he got from wine. The whiskey was hard to get down, but once there it settled like a ship sunk to the ocean's bottom.

With some difficulty he focused on Conrad and said, "You one of them ofay liberals who's got high hopes, but if you stays on this street another week your hopes is gonna just zoom away. Now what you oughta do is go to one of them neighborhoods where the black men live halfway decent and organize them. At least they'll hold still long enough to hear what you gotta say." . . .

"You're unduly harsh, Jackie. These people are no different than any others. All one needs to do is educate them, get them used to different things. They have to identify with what's best for them before they'll accept it. A person can go through his entire life doing the wrong things in the wrong manner; if he's not shown a better way he'll probably keep doing wrong, even if he's harmed in the process." . . .

Jackie took one of Conrad's cigarettes from the pack, and casually put the pack on the bar on the other side of himself, out of Conrad's reach. He felt that chances were good that the man would forget them.

Conrad saw it, and thought it went well with the piece of Howard Street philosophy. Instead of saying anything about it, he
innocently patted his pockets, got up, and went to the cigarette
machine, giving Jackie a chance to put the others away. . . .

. . . "Man," he said, "what you're tryin' to do won't work
around here; but all I can do is tell you. You stick around long
enough and you'll dig it for yourself."

"You could be right, but I have a job to do and I'm going to
keep trying as long as I'm in the area," Conrad said. He then ordered his final drink.

"If I had any money I'd bet you wouldn't last a month. I say
that because you ain't really down—"

"Oh, come off it, Jackie," he interrupted. "Just because I'm
white and not down on my luck doesn't mean—what are you
laughing about?" he ended, showing irritation.

"Because you just tol' me what I mean better 'n I could tell
you. I didn't mean bein' down on your luck. To be *down* is to be
hip, with it—in other words, to know what's happenin', see?"

"Well, I misunderstood you. I thought—"

"That's what I'm talking about!" Jackie said vehemently.
"That's the whole thing with you comin' here. You done misunderstood it all! Dig, you can't understand this hole—you can't
even understand the *talk*—unless you was born and raised here
in it." . . .

Conrad was miffed, but he hid it with a smile. "I may well be
what you call a square, Jackie, but I know—I *dig*, if you like that
better—I dig that people are just people no matter where they've
been raised. No matter what they've been through they can be
taught different. I'm sure that blacks weren't always in the position they occupy in this country; before slavery they had as much
human dignity as anyone else, didn't they? Their actions here
are more of a habit than their nature, isn't that right? So what
they lost during slavery can be regained, can't it? Man is nothing
but man, no matter what his color." . . .

"The longest day of your life, you couldn't dig it, mister,"
Jackie said hotly. "Do you know that if you gave any one of the
people you see a hundred dollars, he wouldn't buy food if he was
hungry? The whores'd give it to their pimps and the men'd go
buy a suit and a pair of long shoes."

"So he'd have twenty left, which his rent would take if he'd
pay it all. But he wouldn't do that; he'd give the landlord maybe
ten, then he'd bring the other ten to Howard Street and party
with it. As for eatin'—he can always beg a sandwich somewhere." . . .

Conrad's head was spinning. He was drunk and he hardly

understood what Jackie was talking about. He ordered two more drinks and vowed to himself that this was his last. . . .

"Now if you still don't believe you're in the wrong neighborhood at the wrong time, man, then you deaf, dumb, and blind. Go on up to them nigger neighborhoods where they wanna be white with black skin and see what you can do for them. Ain't nothin' you can do for us—Look at you, I got you drunk without even tryin'. You a hell of an example, white man!" An angry snap was in Jackie's voice as he looked at Conrad, who wasn't hearing him. He was looking right past Jackie with a meaningless smile on his face. . . .

Conrad didn't understand, and he wasn't even trying now. That last drink had done it to him royally. And he'd been drunk only twice before in his life. He did know that he wanted to leave here, had to get out now. This wino and these people—who were they? They were out to destroy him. . . .

He trembled. He shouldn't think of them as niggers. Ever since he'd joined the CR group he'd honestly tried not to think of them as niggers. They were red-white-and-blue Americans, just like himself. Didn't they fight wars and pay taxes like everyone else? Like himself? But they couldn't be like him. He wanted to help build America, he wanted to obey the law and love his neighbors. These people hated everything, including themselves. They weren't like him. No. No. They weren't like anyone he'd known in his entire life. . . .

He'd go home and sleep it off—couldn't go back to CR headquarters in his present condition. . . . If he felt this way when he woke up again he wasn't going back to CR headquarters at all. . . .

The previous scene might serve as an example of faulty observation—an illustration of the gap that may exist between how an individual sees himself and how he is seen by others and of the disastrous consequences of this kind of distorted vision. Harry Conrad apparently had given no thought at all to how he would look to Jackie Brown and the others on Howard Street. He expected to be seen as he saw himself—a civic-minded young man, better educated and financially placed than they and therefore qualified as a leader of their movement for civil rights. He really believed that his brief education in the civil rights movement had wiped out the color prejudices he had learned from his long exposure to a culture in which he had never known black people but had been conditioned to think of them as inferior in intelligence, self-respect and ability—and dangerous to white people besides. When Harry sat down in the bar to talk with Jackie, he expected Jackie to see him exactly as he presented himself at that moment. When the reality failed to measure up to his expectations, he abandoned the whole project. Derelict though he was, Jackie had a more tenacious hold on his convictions than Harry.

Some of the most effective leaders of community organization efforts were those, unlike Harry Conrad, who had cogent reasons for fearing to join them and ample excuses for avoiding membership.

southern negro college:
ann moody

The following excerpts from the autobiography of a leader in the fight for civil rights gives some insights into emotions with which white people, no matter how sensitive, are usually unfamiliar. Her narrative might have been included in the chapter on children, except that Ann Moody was really never a child. At three years of age, she was already acting as an adult, caring for a younger sister so that her parents could both work in the fields in order to earn enough to keep the family alive. When she was still a little girl, she helped her mother do domestic work in the homes of white people. She saw black people threatened, assaulted, and even murdered while their friends and relatives had to stand silently by or suffer the same fate. She made up her mind young that education was the only avenue out of the life she had been born into and she undertook the long struggle to acquire it.

In the first excerpt below, Ann describes how past experience threatened to interfere with that goal. It also illustrates how human service workers—here white college teachers—may be seen quite otherwise than how they see themselves. In the second, she shows how much courage was required even to join a civil rights organization.

After working her way through all-black high schools and two years of college, Ann won a scholarship to Tougaloo where a high quality of education would be open to her.

> Soon after classes began, I discovered I had only one Negro teacher for the semester. I began to get scared all over again. I had never had a white teacher before. Now I wished I had gone

From *Coming of Age in Mississippi* by Ann Moody (New York: Dial Press), pp. 219, 221. Copyright © 1968 by Ann Moody. Reprinted with the permission of the publisher.

to L.S.U. I knew the whites in New Orleans weren't half as bad as the ones in Mississippi. I kept remembering the ones in my hometown, those that had Samuel O'Quinn murdered, those that burned the entire Taplin family, and those I worked for who treated me like a secondhand dirty dish towel. I got so damn mad just sitting there thinking about those white teachers, chills started running down my back. I knew that if they were at all like the whites I had previously known, I would leave the school immediately.

By this time I had become friendly with my second roommate, Trotter, who was even darker than me. I asked her whether or not she thought I could take it at Tougaloo. If I couldn't, I didn't want to waste my little bit of money.

Trotter laughed and said, "Girl, I had the same feeling when I was a freshman. I came here scared stiff. I didn't know what to expect. I had heard about the white teachers, the high yellow students and all."

"I'm an A student, Trotter, but I've never had any of those tough white teachers. I know I'm going to have some problems."

"No, no, Moody. I came from a little country high school too. Here I am an honor student. You can do the same. All teachers start off pretending they are hot shit. It's the same with Negro teachers. You know that."

"If their disposition is anything similar to the whites in my hometown, I couldn't take that shit either," I said.

"But these teachers here on campus are all from up North or Europe or someplace. We don't have one white teacher here from the South. Northern whites have a different attitude toward Negroes."

"I certainly hope so," I said, relieved of some of my fright. . . .

One night, shortly after Dave and I had broken up, I asked Trotter what kind of meetings she was always going to. She said, "I thought you knew. I'm secretary of the NAACP chapter here on campus."

"I didn't even know they had a chapter here," I said.

"Why don't you become a member? We're starting a voter registration drive in Hinds County and we need canvassers. Besides, it would give you something to do in your spare time, now that you don't see Dave any more."

I promised her that I would go to the next meeting. All that night I didn't sleep. Everything started coming back to me. I thought of Samuel O'Quinn. I thought of how he had been shot in the back with a shotgun because they suspected him of being a member. I thought of Reverend Dupree and his family who had been run out of Woodville when I was a senior in high school, and all he had done was to get up and mention NAACP in a sermon. The more I remembered the killings, beatings, and intimidations, the more I worried what might possibly happen to me or my family if I joined the NAACP. But I knew I was going to join, anyway. I had wanted to for a long time.

In the years before the development of large community programs in deprived areas, employment services were usually located with a view to accessibility to employers and were in general regarded as exchanges, bringing together qualified workers with employers who needed employees with particular skills and training. For many years, however, some public employment services have made special efforts to help young people and people with handicaps to qualify for and find jobs. The importance of work commensurate with ability was recognized from the outset by the new programs to improve the life of inner city residents. Human service workers recognized that it is not merely unemployment that is discouraging and damaging to self-respect. A job, even one with good pay, that uses less than a person's ability and gives him no opportunity for promotion affects his view of himself and the way in which others—including his family—see him. Low job status, almost as much as unemployment, whether or not it is his "fault," relegates a man to the status of a child. In this society, this status is coming to apply to working women as well as men. And welfare recipients face strong disapproval for their dependence upon public support to subsist.

At the same time, human service workers, in close touch with many men and women who are not able to find work or are working in jobs beneath their capacities, have noted that it is not usually "laziness" that holds people back, but a lack of self-confidence which deepens with every additional employment rebuff until they may even stop trying to find work. Suitable employment, then, might go far to solve other problems if people could be helped to try once again to prepare themselves for work and to find and hold jobs. With a view toward helping them to do this, some employment offices have been moved out of midtown facilities where they had been placed chiefly as a convenience to employers, and into the neighborhoods where the people who need jobs live. They are staffed with human service workers trained in vocational counseling, psychology, and social work. And they also have human service workers without special training who have a firsthand knowledge of the neighborhood, the feelings and needs of the people who live there, and ways of helping them to find and hold jobs.

inner city employment service: sheila

The following is a glimpse into the operation of a new kind of neighborhood employment facility that was supported by public funds and focused on helping people prepare themselves for employment, apply for it, and keep it.

Outside the July sun gilded the boarded-up stores, the rotting tenements, and the empty lots where the sun only adds a stench to the scenery that causes Brownsville's residents, bitterly, yet still with some affection for their neighborhood, to refer to it as Biafraville.

Inside, on the ground floor of the modern Neighborhood Manpower Service Center on Rockaway Avenue—one of 20 such job finding and training placement centers operated by the City's Human Resources Administration—more than a hundred black and Latin teenagers crammed themselves into every inch of space, hoping for a summer job.

The Center is a place of hope. On one wall the faces of Malcolm, Althea Gibson, Martin Luther King and other Negro heroes stare gently or fiercely out from a map of the U.S. on which they are superimposed. A hand-scrawled poster advertises City University reading courses tied in with the Center's program for Brownsville dropouts.

In a Peanuts cartoon someone has tacked up, you sense the empathy of the young staff, mostly Brownsvillians themselves who, through in-service university training and experience in trying to awaken stifled ambitions, have become sophisticated vocational counselors at 22 and 26. The cartoon says, "There's no heavier burden than a great potential."

By the end of the week, they would have matched more than 1,000 teenagers with jobs in parks, hospitals, City office buildings

Courtesy of the New York City Human Resources Administration, "The Promise of a Job," from the *Annual Report* (New York, 1969), p. 6.

and other sites that would supply job experience and a paycheck. The matching goes on at Centers in all parts of the City.

But the Center's main responsibility is not the summer teen-agers. It is a whole community festering in poverty and running out of hope.

Like most New York ghettoes, Brownsville is filled with young people who die early inside. They were poorly taught or saw too little value in schooling to stay; they have no marketable skills; they have felt the lash of job discrimination; they have given up looking for decent jobs.

At the rate of about 70 a week, the Brownsville Manpower Service Center seeks them out (or they walk in), tests them, finds remedial programs and training slots for them, counsels them, encourages them to speak about their hopes, refers them to jobs, follows them up, gets some of them into college. And obviously cares.

One such Brownsville manpower worker is 26-year-old Carol Brizzi, a totally-involved dynamo with a college degree whose whiteness nobody on the largely black staff seems to pay any attention to. She is Supervisor of Regular Placement and Intake and talks about her work this way.

"We try to work with them where they're at—vocationally, educationally, and psychologically. One of the hardest things is to get these kids to tell you what they really want. At first they all say they want to be auto mechanics. They're afraid to want to be something else. How can you think you want to be a doctor when you've been raised here? In counseling, some of them discover they don't want to lug garbage, and maybe they don't have to.

"Everybody on the staff has somebody special he keeps tabs on. Mine is Sheila. I think about her when I get discouraged.

"Sheila's 19 now. She first showed up about a year ago in the same blue jeans and sandals she wore for months after that. I couldn't believe anyone as tiny as she could be such a rough little kid. She was raised by an aunt after her parents died and she'd been sick a good bit of her life with epilepsy and a rare blood disease. But she was determined to get off welfare. She couldn't stand being dependent, even with a two-year-old child to raise. She used to say, 'It just mess me up.'

"She was almost too far behind to do anything with. She was reading at the third grade level, but she was a firecracker and bright. We got her into a night math and reading program and she pulled herself up several grades in no time.

"You couldn't tell her there was anything she couldn't do. The hardest thing was to persuade her to give up the idea of becoming a nurse. The epilepsy would have made it impossible.

"Well, she finally decided on clerical work and I arranged for her to be interviewed for our Wall Street training program. Not long before, she'd lost out on a part-time job because she showed up in blue jeans. This time I called the Department of Social Services and got her some clothing money and made her come in here before the interview to pass muster. She really looked swell. And she felt swell. She kept hugging this wooly coat she'd bought.

"I got a call later from the woman at Wall Street. Sheila had kept the coat buttoned up tight all during the testing. The lady caught her fanning herself in the hall later with the lapels of the coat and told her she didn't have to worry that she was wearing an old dress. She was being accepted.

"The woman said to me, 'Her reading's a grade low but she's got so much spunk we've got to take her.'

"Now she's almost got her high school equivalency, and she's being accepted into City University's SEEK program. I still keep tabs on her, but I think this kid is going to do all right."

Human service workers based in the community where service users live have the advantage of being able to see at first hand and appreciate the many influences that impinge on the residents. Workers will note that while in deprived neighborhoods some of these influences are negative and make change difficult for neighborhood people, there are also sources of deep strength and potential development which can be mobilized and supported.

Human service workers who choose the community probably should be certain of their own feelings about group participation to be sure that they do enjoy group membership because they will be in constant contact with groups of people in their work. They will also need the patience to work over long periods of time as change occurs very slowly in group settings. Most of all, they will need to be able to derive personal satisfaction from knowing that they have been influential in bringing about change, since, the more skillful their work, the more invisible they will be. If the workers have done their job well, the natural leadership, individually or collectively, will believe that they themselves have accomplished the task and the community at large will look to them in the future rather than to the workers. All human service workers, especially those in the community, need to be people who can continue to carry out a demanding task without much public recognition or openly expressed gratitude from the recipients of their services.

questions

Both Butch at the RYC and Conrad in Howard Street discovered racial prejudices in themselves they had not known were there. Compare how each of them responded to this new view of themselves and speculate on how it will affect their future actions.

Decode the argument about whether or not Spanish or English was to be spoken at The Puerto Rican Action Committee meeting and describe the issues underlying the argument.

What similarities and differences can you observe between Ann Moody in the rural South and Sheila in the urban North? How would your observations influence your actions as a human service worker?

Community action programs have been severely criticized by many people. State some of these criticisms and your views about them.

additional reading

Stalvey, Lois Mark. *The Education of a WASP*. New York: Viking Press, 1971. This is an autibiographical account of the way in which a family of secure middle class background and status "discovered" themselves to be part of the racist majority and the steps they took to change their own attitudes and to try to change those of others. Their efforts to learn and to act in accordance with their new understanding of their own society resulted in an entirely new way of life for the entire family and to a new and painful awareness of what needs to be done if all American families are to be "free and equal." Perhaps because her introduction to the real nature of racism was so sudden for the college trained, socially secure author, she is pessimistic about the prospects of real change, but it is evident that she and her whole family see working toward that goal as a most important and worthwhile endeavor for others as well as for themselves.

Clark, Kenneth and Jeannette Hopkins. *A Relevant War Against Poverty*. New York: Harper & Row, Harper Torchbooks, 1970 and New York: Metropolitan Applied Research Center, 1968. This study describes the war on poverty programs in twelve cities and compares and rates them in a number of ways. Its purpose is described in the foreword as "strengthening and increasing the effectiveness of anti-poverty programs . . . in the spirit of helping to ensure a serious and relevant war against poverty."

The human service worker interested in community action programs will find here observations about program issues and professional opinions about the reasons for their success and failure which will help him to make some decisions about his place in this interesting, difficult, and rapidly changing area of human service.

8 | *the human service worker and institutions*

In point of numbers, there are today probably more human service people—givers and users—in institutions than anywhere else. There is every reason to believe that in the next decade there will be more human service workers in institutional services than ever before, although there is a trend toward new kinds of services to replace the enormous mental hospitals, schools for the mentally retarded, and correctional facilities which already exist. These institutions may change in character and those living there may stay for increasingly brief periods of time in the future. In this chapter, some of the users and givers of human services under institutional auspices will be presented.

Human service institutions reflect their historical past in ways which may profoundly influence the present for those who live and work in them. This statement warrants a short introduction to institutions in general.

Centuries ago, in European cities, the poor, the sick, the insane, and the criminal were all seen as dangerous by the more fortunate members of society. Society isolated the dangerous elements into institutions and attempted to impress them with the error of their ways so that they would not repeat their behavior on release. It was believed that those already deviant should be made an example of in order to inhibit deviance by others who were tempted to wrong doing. Deprivation, public and private punishment, lack of creature comforts, humiliation, and pain were the tools for achieving the goals of the early congregate institutions. The people who made use of these tools were those who could find satisfaction in doing so— jailers, guards, and others who were often almost as poor, as mad, or as criminal as those they were chosen to "keep."

During epidemics, as some understanding of contagion became widespread, those with recognizable and contagious illness and the very poor were cared for in hospitals, often apart from the jails which housed many who were ill with less recognizable ailments.

As knowledge about human behavior grew, and respect for human life developed, compassionate individuals, often under the leadership of the church, began to recognize and provide for individual differences among the miserable inhabitants of the jails and pesthouses. Special institutions were built to house the poor, the orphaned children, women unable to care for themselves, and those of both sexes whose mental capacities were either permanently or temporarily deficient or deranged. Illness was increasingly understood and cures for the sick sought, often in the hospitals which replaced the first pesthouses as places where people might be helped to live as well as to die, and where doctors could learn more about their profession through observation and experiment.

The first settlers in this country, because their numbers were so limited, had little need for the kinds of large congregate institutions of miserable people that still were to be found in their native cities in the old world. Offenders against the rigid rules of the colonies could be dealt with individually at first. The poor, the handicapped, and the dependent could be "farmed out" to the care of more competent citizens who were paid small sums from public revenue to care for them—though not in a manner to encourage others to thriftlessness and idleness. By the time institutions of any size were built here, they were already serving somewhat differentiated populations. The early nineteenth century saw the organization of poorhouses, institutions for orphaned children, insane asylums, and hospitals. By the middle of the century it was recognized that children might not be entirely at fault for their delinquencies and that they might become upright citizens if they were cared for apart from hardened criminals and retrained in law-abiding habits and marketable skills. Special training and "industrial" schools were organized for this purpose. Prisons continued to be frankly punitive in intent, although in some instances, there were efforts to improve the living conditions in them.

Many of the first institutions were organized under religious auspices, as expressions of Christian principles of compassion, forgiveness, and dedication. The men and women who served as the staff of the institutions lived in them, or close by, and shared in the lives of the inmates. As secular groups and government began to take over the major burden of care, the pattern of shared living arrangements for staff and inmates was largely continued. Staff quarters were often built into the institution's plan, with room and board constituting a large share of the salary for employees. The staff of institutions for children were thought of as parent substitutes. They most often lived with the children to give them the firm guidance their own parents had been unable to provide.

Individuals interested in serving a particular group of people—the aged, the sick, or the young, for example—might have joined a religious order which ministered to that group or sought to work with a comparable secular organization. In times of economic hardship, institutions attracted workers because of the customary provision of room and board. At other times, institutions drew workers because they employed people who lacked formal education or technical skills which would equip them for more highly paid employment. Institutions have always attracted human service workers who have interest and talent in working with people gained from their life experience but without market value elsewhere. And work in institutions, especially correctional institutions, has always appealed to a few who like to control and correct others.

The trend toward urban life caused living conditions to become more crowded, and families had less space to care for members who were physically or emotionally handicapped. Thus, as institutions became more humane, more and more people came to reside in them. From realistic considerations of cost and from some deep fears of contamination, institutions were built in more-or-less isolated surroundings. For many years, individuals once committed to them would live out their lives there in a small world made up of their peers and the human service staff. It was an empty, dull world for both, pushing those already isolated by their handicaps further and further inward, and those isolated by their work into a tightly knit group with its own customs and conventions. The human service workers directly responsible for the residents of the institutions greatly outnumbered specialists, so that while they were not legally responsible for the operation of the institutions, they did in fact create the climate in which thousands of people lived out their lives.

As scientific knowledge grew, this trend was reversed in general hospitals, where highly trained professionals had constant contact with the patients. Hospitals were located where they were accessible to patients, professionals, and scientific resources. Untrained human service staff were mainly employed in ancillary services—housekeeping duties not directly related to patient care.

Today, medical advances have almost eliminated the need for some kinds of hospitals—those for tuberculosis and contagious disease. Hospital stays in general are for briefer periods of time. Improved health services have increased life expectancy so that there are fewer orphans needing care, and better understanding of personality development has led to the predominant use of adoption and foster care, rather than institutionalization for children.

But most important has been the increased prominence that has been given to *people*—to human relationships as a basic tool. This awareness has led to the maintenance of many slightly deviant individuals in the community, who in the past might have been removed from it, and the return to the community of others at a much more rapid rate than used to be the case. At the same time, it has greatly increased the value placed on the relationships that go on inside institutions between those who live there and those who care for them. Good working relationships among human service workers who have different kinds of training and responsibility are also seen as having great importance to the creation of an institutional climate that points toward health.

Normally, human beings move from relationships with one or two close family members to a few more with other children and relatives, and then to the wider world of school and work, maintaining relatively small numbers of close relationships at any one time in their lives and a wide circle of acquaintances. In institutions, an effort is being made to parallel this kind of normal ratio to a greater degree than ever before. Therefore, while the trend is to limit the number of inmates in institutions, there is also an expanded use of human service workers in them although today staff rarely reside in institutions. There are probably more human service workers employed per institution than ever before, and their work is more interesting and varied.

Most of those who are responsible for institutional management agree that very large congregate institutions should be replaced with smaller ones where personal relationships can be more easily carried on. But it is unrealistic to suppose that this can be done at once. The cost of replacing the big hospitals, correctional institutions, and specialized schools would be enormous. Some institutional administrators have partially solved the problem by setting up self-contained units inside the larger whole which help to carry out some of the objectives of a small setting. In many institutions there is a lively recognition of the importance of personalizing the human services by increasing relationships between staff and inmates and among the different levels of staff.

But like all other human services, institutions today reflect their past. In every hospital for the physically or mentally ill or handicapped, in every correctional institution, traces remain of customs and routines that are part of their institutional heritage, of a time when attitudes were more restrictive and more punitive than present policy. Differential treatment of those who can pay their way and those who cannot, meal time and bed time routines, insistence on conformity with the group for its own sake, forms of address between patients and staff, all these aspects of institutional life are often carryovers from the past. They may be so familiar that they go unnoticed and unchanged by institutional administration, but inmates and staff may feel them.

This is not to say that institutional routines should be abolished. Such a move would lead to unlivable chaos for everyone involved. Where numbers of people live in close proximity to each other, there must be rules and routines which are for their protection and which, at the same time, assure their freedom from interference from others. Human service workers in institutions must be able to accept the limits of a firm structure if they are to make helping relationships with the people they care for within the structure. Often, these are people who outwardly resent and test out the limits but who, in fact, need both a structured environment and a helping, personal relationship if they are to make the greatest use of their natural potential. At the same time, institutional workers cannot allow themselves to become too routinized and to lose sight of the individuals they care for. In institutions there is a tendency for daily life to become more and more regulated. Of course, it is always easier for staff to refuse individual requests for small adjustments in program and to think of inmates as a collective "they," than it is to see and respond to individual needs and suffering. But it is more rewarding to see people improve rather than sink into bored monotony and to know that personal attention has helped to restore in them a sense of self-worth and independence.

residential treatment center: wayne

Wayne, like most of the children who come to residential treatment centers for children today, had had unsuccessful and unhappy relationships with his parents which made him anticipate the same kind of treatment from all the other adults he met. He had developed ways of getting the attention all children want and, simultaneously, of "getting even" for the pain adults had inflicted on him in the past. He brought these habits with him to the treatment center where he was provocative, disobedient, and generally hard to get along with. But there is no doubt that he succeeded in being noticed! One would not expect it to be a quick or easy task to develop a friendly relationship with Wayne and Mr. and Mrs. Snyder did not find it so. However, as they acted out their willingness to help, and at the same time showed their interest in Wayne by setting firm limits to the behavior they would tolerate from him, he became more willing to lower his defensive armor and let them see his unhappiness and need for their help and acceptance.

Institutional care was requested for Wayne because he was unable to remain in his own home or to use foster care. Wayne had been badly treated at home by both mother and stepfather. His natural father was dead. He had to eat meals in a separate room; he was rejected in favor of his sister and half sister. He was not permitted to accompany the family on auto trips or to have opportunities to participate in activities with peers. Wayne had been made to feel he was stupid and could do nothing that was right or acceptable to his parents. He could not face his mother's rejection and still felt quite close to her. Every birthday or holiday found him buying her a gift. He is hostile toward all adults because he was removed from his home and says he hopes to see the day when his stepfather and anyone else responsible for having him removed from his home is sorry.

Wayne had been with us only a few days when we felt war had been declared. The tactics he resorted to were infantile. He tattled on the other boys. It was a great achievement for him to get someone else in trouble. He would mimic them and when he could find no other means of annoying them he would simply stand in front of them with his arms folded, staring at them. He had other habits such as burping in the other boys' faces, urinating on the toilet paper in the bathrooms, sneaking away from the table, and emptying his cereal out of the window when we weren't looking.

Wayne's favorite trick was trying to play one houseparent against the other. For example, if he asked to go some place and I felt this was not right for him, I would say, "I'm sorry, Wayne, but I do not approve of your going there and I am sure Mr. Snyder would not approve either." He would then go to Mr. Snyder when I was not around and say, "Mrs. Snyder said if you approved, I can go."

Another way of Wayne's was to follow me around for hours, especially when I was busiest, and just stand and stare. Any attempt at conversation failed. Finally one day I said, "Wayne, why are you doing this?" His answer was, "I'm just trying to get something on you, just waiting for you to make a mistake." My reply was, "Well, just keep waiting. I'm sure I'll make a mistake sooner or later because none of us is perfect."

One Saturday it was Wayne's turn to do the dishes and he had a lawn to mow at a definite time. We overheard him trying to get

From *Tough Times and Tender Moments in Child Care Work* by Eva Burmeister (New York: Columbia University Press, 1967), pp. 204–208. Reprinted with the permission of the publisher.

one of the boys to do this chore for him, but he was not having any success. We volunteered to do this for him because we always try to show all the boys we are here to help when they need us. This was quite strange to Wayne, but from that day on he began to improve. He told us later he felt we were beginning to understand him.

Another incident helped to give me a better insight into Wayne's feelings. One afternoon he was sitting around, just staring into space. I decided to try to occupy him by asking him to play a game of basketball with me. As we bounced the ball around, Wayne began to talk about home. He said he could go home the second week-end in the month if he wanted to, but he had decided he would not. I asked him if there was a reason why he didn't want to go home on this particular week-end. He said rather offhandedly, "No, there is no special reason but my stepfather told me the last time I was home that he was taking my mother away for Thanksgiving and Christmas. So I guess I won't be able to go home for either holiday." I didn't quite know how to answer him, but I did say that I was sorry that he wasn't going home.

I thought quite a bit about the conversation with Wayne and began piecing together other snatches of conversation I had heard from Wayne since his last visit home. I knew that the last time he was home his visit had not gone well. Wayne's parents had told the caseworker that he had not behaved well. Finally I started putting two and two together and realized that this was Wayne's father's way of spiting or punishing him. My heart really ached for Wayne and I knew that he could not admit to himself or anyone else what was really bothering him.

The next afternoon we received a call from school authorities saying that Wayne had misbehaved and they would like to have us speak with him. When we asked what the trouble was they said Wayne had behaved in an infantile manner. When he came home from school we confronted Wayne, and he denied each report. "I didn't throw an eraser. I didn't stick my tongue out at the teacher." We quietly told him that it seemed strange that the teacher would take time out from his busy schedule to call us with false information. Wayne did not answer to this but abruptly changed the subject. He said, "The reason I can't go home for Thanksgiving or Christmas is that my stepfather and mother are going away on business. They *have* to go!"

Right then I realized that I had been correct about Wayne's feelings toward his home. Of course, his parents not wanting him home for the holidays had hurt him, but right now he was trying to tell me that this was the cause of the way he was acting. I hesitated before answering Wayne, and then said, "Wayne, when a person can admit what is bothering him, it's often the best thing in the world for him, because he can then begin to deal with the problem." He then asked me if I knew what was wrong with him. I said I thought I knew and he asked me to tell him. I just didn't feel that it was the time for me or that I was equipped to interpret or handle Wayne's reaction to my answer, so I said, "I think it's better for you to try to find that out for yourself, Wayne." He then asked me if he came to me when he found out what was wrong, would I tell him if I agreed with him. I told him yes. Two weeks have gone by and we are still waiting for Wayne to come to us. We feel sure that when he can really admit his problem, his behavior will improve. We also told the caseworker what had taken place and asked for help with Wayne for this.

Wayne is improving in many ways. He has stopped some of his infantile behavior, but much has to be done with the hostility he feels toward his stepfather and mother and their rejection of him.

It is not difficult to see that if Wayne had remained at home, constantly excluded from full participation with the rest of his family, reminded almost hourly of his "outsider" status even with his own mother, acting out the feelings this situation aroused in him, he would soon have been in very serious difficulties. There was no basis for an agency to step in and bring the problem to court unless Wayne committed a delinquent act because he was not demonstrably neglected at home. And even if he had been placed in a foster home at the request of his parents or court order, it is unlikely that a foster mother would tolerate the kind of behavior he showed when he first entered the group home. Even the Snyders found his behavior almost unbearable and they had the support of the other members of the staff and the satisfactions of success in dealing with some of the other boys.

In the institutional setting Wayne could be observed: in his interaction with others, in his moody withdrawal into his own unhappy thoughts. He could be offered support and understanding in the "doses" needed, at the time and in a way that would not have been possible elsewhere. For a child who had good reason to fear that if he got to like and depend on adults he would be hurt, Wayne could make use of the less personal relationships of the group home to make slow and wary advances in trust to the Snyders and to accept their interest as he could allow himself to let them see how hurt and upset he was.

The Snyders contributed to Wayne's improvement in many ways

although Mrs. Snyder mentions her lack of formal training. While they set limits for him they also acted out their willingness to help him when he needed help. They were consistent in their response to him. And although it must have been hard they were able to wait out some of Wayne's provocative behavior and listen to his obvious lies about his home and family until he himself felt able to begin to let them see how miserable he was and how much he wanted and needed help. At the same time, Mrs. Snyder asked for help from more highly trained staff members when she recognized that Wayne might be severely upset when he talked about his real feelings about his family.

Since other staff members would deal with the boys when the Snyders were off duty or on vacation, the Snyders probably kept some form of daily record, a daily log, so that others might know what to expect. Being busy people, their notes were perhaps quite brief yet they would serve several useful purposes other than giving information for the next people in charge of the group. The necessity to think about Wayne—and every other boy in the group—in order to make some notes about him would help them to focus, however briefly, on his behavior that day—which in the course of busy weeks might otherwise have gone unnoted, especially when it began to improve! Rereading their own notes later would permit the Snyders to review their handling of Wayne, to identify what had been successful or had not, to see how much he had changed through their efforts and to help them in dealing with another boy who showed similar characteristics.

Institutions of all kinds are usually short-handed. While they recognize the importance of individualized services, financing is not often sufficient to permit them to provide it. For this reason, administrators are often glad to make use of volunteers who have the time and interest in working with a special group or who want to test out their aptitudes for such work. It is a fair exchange. The institutionalized population has stimulating contacts with generally enthusiastic and interested "outsiders" and the volunteer has a first hand learning opportunity. As has been suggested, summer vacation times are often well used in such volunteer efforts.

children's hospital: andrea

Andrea describes herself and her motivation for volunteering her summer free time.

Early in the summer of 1967, I looked for a paying job until I had exhausted every possible means of obtaining one. The only real offer I had was to babysit for a 5-year-old, and I decided that I would rather die than stay with one small child for the whole summer. So it was really a last resort that brought me to the Happy Hills Hospital as a junior volunteer.

When I came out to register I was determined to make what could have easily been a twice a week volunteer stint into a full-time job with some value. I had never liked children very much, but since they had always taken to me quite well, I felt that I could do them no harm. When I was told that I would be allowed to work with a 4-year-old problem child with a speech defect, my spirit of adventure was ignited and the job no longer seemed dull.

I met Tommy, my charge, that very day. Tommy is a very handsome little boy to whom you can endear yourself right away. When I had him out on the playground, I thought to myself, "He's no problem; these people must not treat him right." About the same time that I was thinking that, I noticed it was time to come in. When I proceeded to tell Tommy this, he had such a tantrum that I began wondering why they didn't keep him behind bars.

Not only was Tommy's behavior problem greater than I had thought, but so was his speech trouble. In an effort to help him, I went to the library and took out all the books I could get on speech therapy and read them from cover to cover.

For the next 2 weeks, Tommy and I tested each other on just how far the other would go without breaking. By the middle of July, we knew each other quite well and began to develop the first strings of an emotional involvement. For example, Tommy felt I was his property and no one else could have me. I became terribly protective of him. Whatever happened, it just wasn't Tommy's fault.

My attempts at speech therapy turned out to be games in which Tommy learned the correct pronunciation of all the consonants and letter combinations. By the end of the summer, he could pronounce them well, but he still could not see that the same sounds he made in a game should be used in his everyday speech. Although his actual speech was not much clearer than it was when I began working with him, his vocabulary had increased considerably.

In August, a social worker came to talk with Tommy about a

Courtesy of Andrea Levine, "My Experience as a Junior Volunteer" in *Children* 15 (May-June, 1968): 109–110.

foster home. She couldn't understand him at all and so, because I was so proficient, she invited me in. I watched her deal with him and began to see how far he and I had come in learning to communicate with one another. The social worker asked me to try to explain to Tommy that he was going to have a new mommy and daddy. Later Tommy and I talked about it a few times, and he seemed to understand as well as he could for not as yet having met his new family.

One day late in August, I took Tommy to the psychologist at the Sinai Hospital. The psychologist couldn't understand him, so he asked me to come in. The psychologist tried hard to get through to Tommy, asking him all sorts of questions to which I knew Tommy knew the answers, but Tommy was far more interested in the alarm clock and tape recorder than in listening to anyone! But I held my tongue until the psychologist showed Tommy a wagon with a wheel missing and tried to coax him into saying something about it. I just could not be quiet any longer, so I yelled: "Tommy, what's wrong with that wagon?" Tommy looked at me as though I were sick and answered, plain as day, "The wheel's broken."

I think the worst day I had at Happy Hills was the day I came to work just in time to see my Tommy get into a car with his new foster parents. It is rather hard to believe that Tommy isn't really mine and that all I did was to make it easier for him to enter a family. I suppose that that was worthwhile.

I'll miss Tommy a great deal. But I have other ties at Happy Hills. I know all the children there. I've made a lot of friends, and, more important, I've discovered that I can deal with children successfully.

I've always wanted to go into the field of psychology, but I never knew what branch. After last summer's activity, I think I just might have a go at abnormal child psychology. And if I'm successful, I think I'll come back to Happy Hills and do another summer's worth of volunteer work.

general hospital: three views

General hospitals are frequently depicted with glamour in books and on T.V., perhaps because so many crisis situations take place in them. Like other, less well-publicized institutions, they have varying effects on patients and on staff. Some vignettes about general hospitals follow, illustrating some different points of view about them.

teen-age volunteer

A college student in an interview discusses an experience she had at seventeen.

One thing I know I *don't* want to do is be a nurse or be around any kind of sick people. I used to be sure I wanted to be a nurse and so I joined up as a candy striper in a big hospital near where I live when I was a senior in high school. It was volunteer, of course. What we did was kind of fun—we got to take the orders for dinners and then we gave out snacks in the evening. If there was a buzzer we went to see what they wanted. Usually we could do it but we didn't have to give out bedpans or anything like that, but if it was something simple we could do it. That was part of the fun. Like giving out mail which people liked to get.

I was passing out the mail one day and there was a letter for an old man who had never had one before. You know, you become attached to some people in a hospital who are there a long time. There was this very, very old man and everyone kind of ignored him because he was like senile—he couldn't understand or he couldn't hear—I don't really know what his problem was because they said we were not supposed to know about the patients, just do our chores. But I used to kind of talk to him when I had time or brought him a tray or something, but I'd never gotten much response.

So this day I had a letter for him and I told him and he like perked up—it was like he knew it was from his daughter or his granddaughter or something. So I decided, "This really hits him, it's making him happy," so I asked him if he wanted me to read it to him and he gave me the response like yes, and so I read it. It was the most heart warming letter I'd ever read in my life. And the old man started crying, and then me, I started choking up and I couldn't finish reading the letter and he kept looking at me with tears rolling down wanting me to go on—but I just couldn't so I just put it down and rushed into the john and cried. I couldn't stand it. And then, when I went back the next week, this old man had died. And I felt so awful that—maybe if I had finished the letter—to this day I remember exactly what he looked like, his name and everything.

From an unpublished taped interview.

I told the head nurse about it and said I was quitting because I felt so bad and she said OK, because if I was going to be upset by every little thing I'd never last in a hospital, and anyway if I had done what I was told and just handed out the letters this wouldn't have happened and this is the kind of thing that made things hard for the regular nurses. So I for sure don't ever want to work with sick people—I just couldn't stand it.

student nurses

The following discussion took place in a course on human behavior for student nurses in their final year of training.

A: At first, in a hospital you never seem to get to know a person—you're always stirring around trying to get your work done. You don't have time and you don't know how. Maybe now I'll learn to use the time while I'm giving a bath to talk. I think I stopped people from talking it out before—I'd talk about the weather, their family—about everything but what they're there for. It's quicker. It's a short conversation you can end quick.

B: They teach us in class that we're supposed to listen to patients and let them talk but if you do, they can go on for hours. They tell you to think of the patient first when you start in nursing, but you find the ideal and the reality are different.

A: I think before I didn't encourage people to talk because I wasn't sure how to answer them. But now I feel more capable. Well, I mean I may not know what to say, but I can listen and try to understand.

C: You can get away with not talking. The patient is kind of at—your mercy, in a sense. You have nursing procedures to do—you don't have to get involved with a patient.

A: I did social work for a year and I never spent such a helluva frustrating year in my life. I was in Vista on an Indian reservation and I just hated it. Because I went in with an idea I was going to help and I was only nineteen, and they were old and they said how could I help them, and I wonder now what made me think I could tell them anything. It was just a continuous battle all year long. Then, I needed the money so I went to work in a nursing home and I loved old people, just really loved them. So I decided to go into nursing.

C: I had the idea of going into nursing when I was six years old. It didn't turn out the way I thought it would, though, because I guess I never sat down and really thought about what it would be like. And I found I didn't like it as much as I thought I would. . . . It was messy, I didn't like working with the people, and making beds and giving baths and stuff.

B: One of my sisters was a nurse and she used to come home and tell me how it was, the good and the bad. And I guess in comparison with what her other friends did—working in offices, and like that—it sounded a lot more exciting, and interesting.

E: I got started with the idea of nursing when I was young, too. But I wanted more academic background so I went to college first and found out that I like working closer to people. But I know I'll go back to college. One of the things that's hard for me—for twenty or twenty-one years I had developed, you know, how to act like a girl, a woman, and you get these positive responses, so you just keep on doing these things. And then you have this uniform on—like a shell—and that's the way your patient sees you—it's confusing. . . .

patient

The following remarks are taken from a letter by a social worker to a professional journal, corroborating an article which had suggested that professional jargon was a barrier to good communication.

Upon entering the hospital as a patient I found myself in the bed next to a protection client [the mother of a child reported to the social agency as neglected or abused], Mrs. A., whom I had seen on intake a few months previously. As the nurse introduced us, my confidentiality-programmed mind decided to greet the lady with noncommittal recognition. . . .

"Hello there!" I volunteered with suitable warmth. She replied pleasantly, "Remember we met at Children's Aid? My little boy is in an institution now. Mrs. Jones is my regular worker."

Thus, the client established the climate of honest interaction.

I am not a good patient. As I became immersed in the frustrating, dehumanizing hospital ordeal, my "professional self" was drowned in anxiety and fear. . . .

Luckily, my roommate . . . "read me quickly and accurately" and did what she could for me. When I was withdrawn she re-

A letter from Gloria Sewell to "Readers' comments," *Social Casework* 51 (June, 1970): 368.

spected my silence, unwittingly universalizing by commenting later that "everyone likes to be quiet sometimes." Her sympathetic comments were factual, drawn from her own extensive knowledge of hospitals, unhampered by the sifting out of anything which might be labelled "false reassurance." She cheered me with anecdotes of her personal life. . . . I was very grateful for her spontaneous kindness to me in my time of need.

My encounter with Mrs. A was simply an example of how human beings relate to each other with love and encouragement. . . .

These vignettes, which take place in general hospitals, bear out what has been found to be true of most human service settings—they are not easy, romantic places in which to work with happy, grateful people. Individuals react to being there as members of the staff or as patients in many ways. It is increasingly recognized that good and efficient patient care and rapid recovery are related to the amount of personal interest and attention patients receive from staff, as well as to the use of constantly more sophisticated technological equipment. People of many different kinds of personal and professional backgrounds and training work in general hospitals today and will, no doubt, do so in the future, giving a wide choice to individuals interested in the hospital setting.

nursing home:
eric

Patient stays in general hospitals have become much shorter in recent years. The enormous development of skills and knowledge has added so much overhead expense to hospital operation that a long stay becomes prohibitively expensive for most people. Patients with chronic illnesses or incapacities who cannot be cared for at home are therefore often cared for in nursing homes which are rapidly increasing in numbers. A college student, working as an orderly in a nursing home, wrote this account of his contact with one of the patients.

Eric is now forty-one years old. He was born with some facial deformities which are now pretty ugly to look at. He is severely retarded and acts that way.

Eric stayed at home until he was three. It was then decided

From an unpublished report. Used with permission.

that he should attend a special school where he could be with children his age. He remained at the school until he was ten years old. He was doing well but seemed to miss his mother. The school director decided it would be better for him to be at home for a while. At that time, he was six feet one inch tall and weighed 175 pounds. He was constantly harassed by his peers because of his facial deformities.

At eighteen, he tried to kill his mother "for doing this to me," meaning his deformities. He was then committed to a state institution.

With medical care and drugs, Eric's fits of rage were controlled but his physical condition declined and he had difficulty walking and was confined to a wheel chair. Five years ago he was transferred to the ward I work in where there are mostly older, infirm patients. He seems pretty content. He goes to his own "school." Every morning he watches "Sesame Street" on television. He watches TV most of the day sitting in his wheel chair.

october 19

When I talked to Eric today he said he doesn't like it here. He told me that when he was in watching TV on Friday afternoon an old lady came in and pushed him against the wall and hit him with her cane. He said he tried not to get mad because he knows she is "not right" but he hit her anyway. He was punished by having to stay in his room all weekend. I can see that punishment is something needed but I think this was too severe. When I was talking with him, he said "Why do you want to talk to me—I'm so ugly nobody wants to talk to me," and then he cried.

His mother wrote him a letter and I read it to him. She wrote a friendly letter but very impersonal like "How's the weather?" I was surprised that Eric noticed this, too. He didn't want me to write a letter back to her for him. He said, "I don't want her to know I'm alive yet. If I don't write she'll think I'm dead."

november 7

Last week Eric was taken to the general hospital as a result of a fall he had while being moved from bed to his wheel chair. He is glad to be back now but it is hard for him to be in bed all day as he has to be. He looked puzzled when I came in and spoke to him. I got the impression he had forgotten me. He said, "Who the hell are you?" But when I reminded him we had talked before, his face lit up. It's like being in slow motion around him. He takes about three minutes to respond to anything and sometimes longer before he gets it together enough to answer. Being in bed all the time, he finds it interesting to call the aides when they are busy and then saying he forgot what he wanted because they took so long! So he has a sense of humor!

november 23

With the head nurse's permission, I asked the doctor if I could walk Eric a little when I have time. The doctor said, "Sure, great." So I asked Eric if he would like to walk without the wheelchair. He got so excited he was bubbling all over. He said he couldn't remember when was the last time he was on his feet. He did surprisingly well. In fact, I couldn't get him to stop. He bragged to everyone that he is learning to walk again and when I came in a couple of days later he remembered me. I now mean something to him. I told the head nurse I thought it was a shame that nobody was helping him to walk regularly. She said she would get the physiotherapist to reevaluate Eric when he had time.

The physiotherapist says Eric will never be able to walk unassisted and that it would be too dangerous to try to get him to learn to use crutches so I guess he'll stay in the wheel chair. I'm sorry for him—he is such a miserable ugly kind of creature. The nurse has been talking to me quite a lot at coffee break. She asked me all about myself and what I was going to be.

Not so long ago, a mentally ill individual who was committed to a mental hospital or entered one voluntarily remained there for many years, often for the rest of his life. And the same forces of urbanization and mobility that affected other human services increased the rate at which people were coming to mental hospitals. By the middle of this century mental hospitals were often appallingly crowded, and the need for new buildings and additional staff seemed to demand astronomically large financial investment. This situation gave great impetus to reconsideration of the function of mental hospitals, and at the same time, the development of new drugs made it feasible for patients to be safely cared for in the community. As a result, mental hospital populations have declined and can be expected to continue to do so. Nevertheless, almost half a million patients are in mental hospitals on any given day and a quarter of a million people care for them there as psychiatric aides, nurses, doctors, physical and occupational therapists, and in various other capacities. Mental hospitals offer a major employment resource for human service workers of all kinds.

Unlike other hospitals, mental hospitals have often been seen in a negative and even sinister light. Although this view is decreasing, many people still think of the mentally ill in terms of extremes of behavior and the chief task of hospital personnel to be their containment. Some mentally ill individuals do fit the stereotype, of course, but many more resemble those described in the following excerpt from a novel. The major action takes place in a mental hospital and centers about a young woman from a privileged home, Deborah.

mental hospital: deborah

They took Deborah to a small, plain room, guarding her there until the showers were empty. She was watched there also, by a woman who sat placidly in the steam and looked her up and down as she dried herself. Deborah did what she was told dutifully, but she kept her left arm slightly turned inward, so as to hide from sight the two small, healing puncture wounds on the wrist. Serving the new routine, she went back to the room and answered some questions about herself put to her by a sardonic doctor who seemed to be displeased. It was obvious that he did not hear the roaring behind her.

Into the vacuum of the Midworld where she stood between Yr and Now, the Collect was beginning to come to life. Soon they would be shouting curses and taunts at her, deafening her for both worlds. She was fighting against their coming the way a child, expecting punishment, anticipates it by striking out wildly. She began to tell the doctor the truth about some of the questions he was asking. Let them call her lazy and a liar now. The roar mounted a little and she could hear some of the words in it. The room offered no distraction. To escape engulfment there was only the Here, with its ice-cold doctor and his notebook, or Yr with its golden meadows and gods. But Yr also held its regions of horror and lostness, and she no longer knew to which kingdom in Yr there was passage. Doctors were supposed to help in this.

She looked at the one who sat fading amid the clamor and

From *I Never Promised You a Rose Garden* by Hannah Green (New York: Holt, Rinehart and Winston), pp. 15, 99–101. Copyright © 1964 by Hannah Green. Reprinted with the permission of the publishers, Holt, Rinehart and Winston and Victor Gollancz, Ltd., London.

said, "I told you the truth about these things you asked. Now are you going to help me?"

"That depends on you," he said acidly, shut his notebook, and left. *A specialist,* laughed Anterrabae, the Falling God.

Let me go with you, she begged him, down and down beside him because he was eternally falling.

So it shall be, he said. His hair, which was fire, curled a little in the wind of the fall.

That day and the next she spent on Yr's plains, simple long sweeps of land where the eye was soothed by the depth of space.

For this great mercy, Deborah was deeply grateful to the Powers. There had been too much blindness, cold, and pain in Yr these past hard months. Now, as by the laws of the world, her image walked around and answered and asked and acted; she, no longer Deborah, but a person bearing the appropriate name for a dweller on Yr's plains, sang and danced and recited the ritual songs to a caressing wind that blew on the long grasses. . . .

The following episode takes place months later. Hobbs, an attendant the patients did not like, possibly because he was seriously disturbed himself, has died and the nurse is introducing a new attendant to the ward. Knowing how hard they made it for Hobbs, the nurse may herself be somewhat apprehensive and tense. It is interesting to note that the entry into the ward of the well-liked familiar ward attendant, McPherson, dispels the tension as in a few words, he shows the patients that he recognizes them as people like himself.

The evening shift was here, and the patients were all waiting to see who would be taking Hobb's place. When those at the head of the hall saw, they carried the news back.

"It's a Nose—a new one—a new Nose," and there was an almost palpable groan. Noses were Conscientious Objectors who had selected to work in mental hospitals as an alternative to prison. Lee Miller had originated the name "Nose" a long time ago by saying, "Oh, those conchies; I hate them. They won't fight, so the government says, 'We'll rub your noses in it for you! It's either prison or the nut-house!' " Helene had laughed and someone else had said, "Well, they're the noses and we're it."

Now Carla only murmured, "I like being somebody's punishment; it makes me feel needed," and she laughed, but with a bitterness that was rare for her.

The Noses usually came in pairs. "I suppose we should call one of them a Nostril," precise Mary said, rubbing the blood from invisible stigmata. The patients laughed.

"Maybe he'll be all right," Carla said. "Anything's better than Hobbs."

They watched the new staff member go his first long and hard walk down the hall. He was terrified. They saw his terror with feelings caught between amusement and anger. Constantia, in the seclusion section, began to scream when she saw him, and Mary, hearing it, said, "Oh, my God, he's going to faint!" laughing and then hurt: "She's only a *person*, you know."

"He's afraid he'll catch what we have," Deborah said, and they all laughed. . . .

The expedition neared them.

"Get up off the floor, will you please?" the head ward nurse said to the group of patients sitting against the walls of the hall and corridor.

Deborah looked at the Nose. "Obstacle," she said.

She meant that she and the other patients with feet stuck out before the terrified man were like the contrivances in the obstacle courses that men must run through in their military training; that she and they understood their substitution as "the horrors of war," and that they would try to fulfill the Army's desire that this man's training be rigorous. But the nurses neither laughed nor understood, and passed by with another admonition about getting off the floor. The patients all knew that it was merely form. Everybody always sat on the floor and it was only when guests came that nurses, like suburban wives clucked at the dust and wished that "things were neater."

Constantia was beginning to work herself up into an all-night howl, when the ward door opened and McPherson let himself in. Deborah looked hard at him, saw everyone suddenly go easier, and said meaningfully, "They should have changed the lock."

She was thinking that McPherson's key-turn and incoming was a completely different order from the one which had preceded it—as different as if there had been different doors and different locks. She felt obscurely that the words had somehow done her injury, and so she went over them, seeking the culprit.

"They . . . should . . have . . . changed . . . the . . . lock."

McPherson said, "I don't like this key business anyway." Carla looked around, as Deborah had just before, knowing that no one understood, but with McPherson, not understanding carried no penalty of scorn or hatred. She sat back quietly.

They were all glad that McPherson was there, and because feeling this meant that they were vulnerable, they had to try to hide it. "Without those keys you wouldn't know yourself from us!"

But McPherson only laughed—a laughter at himself; not at them. "We're not so different," he said, and went into the nursing station.

"Who is he kidding!" Helene said. There was no malice in her statement; she was merely hurrying to rebuild the wall that he had breached. She turned and disappeared into her limbo, and because McPherson's afterimage still hung in the air there were no catty remarks about her fadeout. But when the procession of magi passed by once more, bearing with them the Nose, rigid and clamp-jawed with fear, no one could withhold the cruelty which seemed to each her true and natural self. . . . Helene shuddered as he passed; Carla looked blank; Mary, always inappropriately gay, trilled laughter.

These scenes portray vividly the terrible confusion of the patients who are sometimes entirely out of contact with their surroundings and at other times are aware of where they are and why. At the same time, they demonstrate how far-reaching the effect may be of a relationship with a human service worker who cares about the patients and understands their problems.

Such concern is nowadays often expressed by the administration through the provision of activities which will relieve the inevitable monotony of hospital life and prevent patients from becoming automatons guided by institutional routines. Perhaps Deborah and the other women on her ward were still too ill to make use of some such activities but a great many patients can profit from them. Though many ancillary mental hospital services need the direction of specially trained staff, there is room in them for the enthusiasm and spontaneity of individuals who have as yet no special training.

state mental hospital: recreation worker

The recreation worker who describes his activities below is one of the new kind of staff that is now being employed by forward-looking mental hospitals. With their enthusiasm and "normality" and some training, such workers have a great deal to offer patients.

My father is a doctor so I had some interest in medicine, but I did not want to take the concentration of courses I needed for pre-med. I enjoyed my psychology courses and considered making that my major. The summer of my junior year I began working at the State Hospital and I continued part time through the winter. Now I'm working full time and then maybe I'll go back and get an MA in psychology. My work here has been supervised by a trained recreational therapist and I may decide to do that instead.

I was pretty scared before I started—there were always a lot of stories going around about the State Hospital and I had never really seen anybody that was mentally ill and I knew they sometimes had murderers and people like that there—dangerous. I figured I would have to be pretty careful—not turn my back on them.

So I came out here and my first day my boss took me to every unit—every ward in this entire hospital he took me to. It took a full day, and he had me meet all the staff and everything because he guessed what my view was, I think. I thought it would be padded cells—and every door would be locked. I couldn't understand why in the world they have patients running around on the grounds. To me, it seemed like it ought to be more like a penitentiary. After the first day I wasn't scared at all.

I've had a few things happen—like once a patient grabbed me just as I got off the elevator and held me tight with my arms pinned and for a minute I felt pretty panicked. But then I looked at him and he was grinning and nodding and I realized he was trying to be nice and affectionate so I just talked to him for a minute and he let go and walked away.

In recreation therapy I do everything with the patients outside of their group projects—any kind of recreation. I like to take some patients that are really emotionally upset and take them into a situation with a group where they won't be able to get into a corner all alone. Or depressives—I like to take them to the gym to play basketball or volleyball where they have to be in a group.

We don't just necessarily go out and play. I set it up so once a week we have an educational tour and then we talk about it, or we have a movie and I take so many patients. I try to get a different group each time. One time we go to the dairy—we show a movie about the dairy before we go—and then we talk about

From an unpublished taped interview.

what things were like different from the movie. There are adults and teenagers.

I just don't work an eight-hour shift straight through. Like a couple of hours at night we have a volleyball tournament, or on a weekend if we're going to have a carnival—no set schedule. I have my own freedom about what I want to do. The only ones I wouldn't work with would be the ones who are restricted to the ward.

There are about ninety people in this unit and that's a lot but you get to know them. That's what makes you feel good—you walk on the ward in the morning and they'll call you by your name. They don't look at me like I'm a doctor or a nurse or a social worker—they look at me as something totally different. Some of them will sit down and talk to me and they know I haven't all that training. They think of me just as a friend of theirs. They don't expect me to help them out. They just tell me their problems and we just sit and discuss it. Of course, I don't wear any white coat or anything. We had a dance a couple of weeks ago and this one man wanted me to let him out and I said, "I'm sorry, but I can't let patients out," and he said, "But I'm the staff!"

It's slow sometimes, and you have to have patience. I took this one girl out who was really nervous and upset with herself. She's slow in her reflexes. I took her out to play volleyball last night and the ball comes to her and she doesn't know what to do with it so she just freezes. Now the patients are just upset with her because she's losing the game for them. So they're telling me to take her out of the game. I always use an excuse when something like this happens that I don't have anyone to substitute for her so she'll have to stay in unless you would like to go out of the game and find someone. "Oh, no, I don't want to do that." So it's OK. . . .

It's hard when you see patients that don't get better—we don't see many on this unit. But there is one man—he was here last summer and he's still here and I don't know what I can do. I've done a lot of studying to see what I could change with him but nothing seems to help so far. Because last summer he was just really active. He's really good at any kind of recreation that he did and this summer he doesn't want to do anything, and when he does do it he's really not doing it. We play softball and he wouldn't even try to hit the ball. If he hits it, he runs to first base but he doesn't like to run any more, so he'd rather just get out. But I just keep trying—I'm not the type to give up.

One of the most interesting and most baffling aspects of the human services is that generalizations about them, like most generalizations, are unsafe! It is true that routines and repetition become stultifying and distressing to many people in institutions.

In many correctional institutions this is especially true since the inmates in general are well aware of the long, empty repetitious days and years still to be faced. The terrible sameness of every day is seen by most inmates of all kinds of correctional facilities as one of their most negative features.

Yet, paradoxically, for a few, these routines have a different effect, offering them a sense of security and the assurance of care that they may never have experienced before.

A certain amount of routine, for a very small child, gives him a sense of safety, a feeling that he can count on being fed, changed, put to sleep. A very young child is entirely dependent on others for survival—if they do not provide him with these essentials he will not survive. So their provision regularly permits him to assume that they will continue to be provided, that he can depend on his small world to take care of him.

Unfortunately, many parents have so many problems of their own that they are unable to care for their children consistently with the kind of dependable regularity that small children need to feel safe. Many young children are still cared for by a succession of people, each having a different style, each, perhaps, not aware of the earlier experiences of the child and not prepared to offer him what he needs.

An adult who has never had the kind of consistent loving care most people take for granted may find a kind of facsimile of such care in an institution. It may even be true that some of the recidivism (repetitions of offenses that return ex-prisoners to institutions) may be silent expression of an individual's belief that life where one's needs are automatically cared for even under conditions that others find intolerable, is preferable to one where he has to fight the world alone, with weapons that seem as inadequate as those of a young child.

minimum security prison: joe

Joe was one of those who found a correctional institution a haven. He talked freely and often to a counselor at the minimum security prison where he was working out a three-year sentence for robbery. The following is a composite of some of these talks which were tape recorded with his permission.

JOE: This isn't the worst place I lived—I been around a lot of places since I was a little kid.

COUNSELOR: Where did you live when you were little?

JOE: St. Elizabeth's orphanage. I was raised up there for the time being. I don't really know how long. I was about eight—no, maybe smaller when I left to my first foster home. That's where I got my fingers removed from—I had an accident over there, at St. Elizabeth's.

COUN: What happened?

JOE: Umm—I was maybe, two, three years old. I got them cut off in a clothes wringer. I was playing around, just stuck my finger in there and zung! That was it. I went to the hospital for it. Must have been Christmas—I remember the Sisters came around and told me to say Merry Christmas.

COUN: And from there—

JOE: I went to my first foster home and then on to the one on 10th Place and from there to Spring Road, and then right back to St. Elizabeth's.

COUN: How come so many places?

JOE: Well, the first one was bad reports, the way I was being treated, me and my two sisters. The woman, she had four kids of her own and they got everything. I remember I used to steal other kids lunches in school, and stuff. So they moved me. And that's where the school trouble started. Because when it came time for me to do homework, I never did do it.

COUN: What were you doing instead?

JOE: Having fun. I was a kid so what I had was fun in a kid's way.

COUN: Well, sometimes when kids goof off in school they have fun but sometimes they're not really having so much fun. You were enjoying yourself?

JOE: At times I guess I was, and at times I guess I wasn't. There in that new place I was the only child in the family. It was pretty hard for me. I was alone in the afternoons. Saturdays and Sundays she gave me extra work to do after doing my homework on Fridays. I started there in the fifth grade and I started cutting up in class and everything. I got through the fifth and then I was cutting class and getting mixed up with girls.

COUN: You were mixed up with girls when you were eleven?

JOE: Yeah, I never did fool with girls—I was serious. I knew all about it before, even before I got to this age. I knew at the time what the grown-ups was talking about and why they were talking about it. I just listened. Let it soak in and I thought I'd try it on somebody. A lot of kids was scared of me. I'd get angry and beat them up but I never did beat up on a girl—I had it in mind but I never did. I'd think of a lot of ways of getting even with them. Some of them gave in to me. And that's why I got sent to Boy's Village. The judge gave me an extra year there. After the detention cottage—it's like a training school—you go to the regular cottage—I was in number eleven. It's called an open cottage—you were free. You know, you could run around the campus, play ball, play ping-pong, cards, and so on. You weren't old enough to smoke so you didn't smoke around there, but you had all kinds of activities and sports. And they make sure you have eight hours of sleep nights. Every day, get up, clean up the cottage, go to school, eat lunch, clean up and then when school is over, everybody goes outside, play softball, football, just fool around. Play cards or checkers, watch TV until it's time to go to bed. Everybody takes a shower every night before you go to bed—they change the sheets on your bed every week, and your pajamas—

My cottage parent was the best. He understood my ways. He would take me up to his grandfather's farm with him. I was the only one he trusted to clean his rooms where he and his wife and children stayed. They leave money around, I never messed with it, you know.

COUN: You liked that place.

JOE: It made you feel like you was home. To me, anyway, because I didn't have no home. I felt kind of free, everybody treated me nice. And if you was wrong, you know, they let you know and they'd try their best to help you out. Give you a chance. Understand your ways. They just made things real nice. I was recommended for everything that came up, like week-end home and for holidays—but I couldn't go because I had no place to go.

COUN: Where are your parents?

JOE: I don't know. I guess if it weren't for me, nobody in my family would have knew where my mother was ever. While I was down there we had social workers and I asked mine if I could find out where my mother was. I had never seen her before but I was curious to see what she looked like. I wanted to ask her different questions. So he said he would try and he called the Department of Public Welfare and had her traced and everything. So when I left and went to the court the judge said my case was dismissed and that's where my mother came. That's where they told her to come there to meet me. And so finally after I met her I didn't have nothing to say to her. She usually lived over on Bay Street. I used to go over now and then to see how she was. Then I was told to stop going down there because she had TB. So I stopped for a while and then I heard she moved to a street closer to me so I started sneaking down there. Both my sisters can't stand her and she don't like both my sisters nor my brother neither.

COUN: Is she better now?

JOE: I don't know. She moved again and I haven't seen her since.

COUN: Couldn't you find her through the Welfare Department again?

JOE: Never asked. Let well enough alone. I decided she didn't want to be bothered with me.

COUN: Did you ever ask your mother about your father?

JOE: I asked her when I first saw her, I asked her what happened to him and she told me he got killed, got shot. And that was it. She was carrying me, and some man come up and was messing around with her, so my father was trying to break it up so the man shot him. . . .

I just sort of lost interest all together when I got back. I used to go to school and go to sleep, or cut, do anything. I got put out. It was my fault in a way but I blame the teacher, too. Had a fight with him but I went back next day and apologized but I still got put out. So I started hanging around, drinking nights, you know, coming in drunk, fighting—tried pot, bennies, speed.

Once I went to see my brother where he was boarded with a lady on Carmel Street. She was nice and I asked her could she find me a place and she did. . . .

So I started looking for a job. I was up every day early in the morning until late in the afternoon but I didn't find nothing. Night time I used to roam around the street, looking for new kicks. I had myself a regular routine—stay in bed until twelve o'clock, get up, listen to the radio, long about four o'clock I'd go look at TV until about seven, go out a while and maybe hustle some stuff, go to bed. Tried to get in the Army when I was seventeen but I couldn't pass the tests. Then I tried again and I passed all right but the doctor threw me out when he saw my hand. Told him it never bothered me but they wouldn't take me. So I hung around some more. I grabbed a woman's purse one night and she wouldn't let go—started screaming—slugged her but the cops were right there for once.

What the social worker hears and reads into Joe's account of his past cannot lead to a very optimistic view of his future. But the social worker no doubt did note that Joe was eager to talk about himself, an attitude that signaled his trust that he would be understood. This had perhaps developed through his association with the cottage supervisor at the training school, the social worker who helped him find his mother—even though that quest ended in yet another rejection for Joe—and in the boarding house lady who took him in. The social worker might recognize that the time Joe must spend in the present institution should be devoted to widening his ability to trust others, and himself. This would, no doubt, require that in addition to positive contacts with human service workers he would have the opportunity of acquiring marketable skills and some practice in making use of them under the burden of suspicion that he is likely to encounter in the community when he is returned to it. At the present time, some correctional institutions have work release and post release programs in communities which allow for a transitional period for individuals like Joe who would otherwise find the demands of total independence coupled with the stigma of being an "ex-con" too much to handle.

Even with a great deal of support and the acquisition of employable skills, it would be unrealistic to expect that Joe would leave the correctional facility for a totally successful future. Without the investment of a great deal of human concern and technical training, however, his future is unfortunately reliably predictable as one of continuing unhappiness and a life of more or less continuous confinement at tremendous public expense.

Only a few years ago, it would have been unnecessary to mention human services with individuals suffering from alcohol or drug addiction. They were usually an undifferentiated part of the population of correctional, mental health, or chronic disease facilities. Detention was the major form of treatment offered them. It consisted largely of enforcing total abstinence. There were a few specialized public and private institutions that attempted further treatment chiefly through physiotherapy or chemotherapy with the aim of reducing the symptoms and returning the addict to the community as rapidly as possible.

Today, all these forms of treatment are in use but there is also a growing recognition that the dimensions of the problem require other, more effective means. There is growing dependence on the establishment of a personal relationship between the addict and a human service worker as the key to success with all forms of treatment. Many human service workers, trained and untrained, are being recruited to work with the sharply increased numbers of addicted people. Although many of these programs are based in the community on an outpatient plan, most of them have some connections with institutions. For this reason, they are dealt with in this chapter.

There is no doubt that work with addicts makes great demands on human service workers. The addicts themselves are difficult to work with. They are often undependable and unpredictable and may cause themselves and others injury and unhappiness. The general public complicates the work of the human service worker with addicts. Part of the public blames the worker because he is not strict and punitive and another part is critical because he is interfering with a valid and harmless life style. Fortunately, the worker can take some satisfaction in knowing that he is a pioneer in work which affects a very large number of people at every social level.

addiction treatment clinic: staff

Because the expansion of services for addicted individuals has been so rapid, there are few workers available who have had training or long experience in this field. Workers have therefore been recruited from a variety of backgrounds and are testing out a number of different treatment approaches. Some members of a staff made up of such individuals were asked to talk a little about themselves, how they had come to be at the clinic, and their impressions about their work. The clinic, a service of a state mental health department, was housed in a downtown office building.

A. I'm a rehabilitation counselor. I have a master's degree in vocational rehabilitation. Where I was before, I had a case load of mostly physical disabilities. The mentally ill were pretty few in the office I was in and I never had much to do with alcoholics or drug users. At least I didn't know it if I did.

B. I was majoring in sociology in college and I took a course in alcoholism and got real interested in it. First I volunteered to work here and then I got a regular job for this summer and now I'm not sure I'll go back and finish college. I like this type of work and I have what I need to do it now, I think.

C. I'm a RN and I never had any experience with alcoholics in my training and when I got through I did pediatric nursing. But a doctor I know was working here and asked me if I would fill a job they had open. It scared me but I'm real curious and I got to wondering about what in the world goes on in the heads of people who seem to deliberately hurt their health with drugs or alcohol.

A. I've been pretty frustrated by this work—I guess because I try to use my own life style to understand these people. Like I thought I was doing real well with a drug user—he was coming in regularly and talking to me in a very friendly way about hating his addiction—and then I found out that all the time he was pushing drugs. You sure have to have an awful lot of patience because you're going to meet more defeat than you are success.

C. I don't really feel all that frustrated. I find many of them delightful people. Some of them struggle hard and some of them are lazy and give up easy just like other kinds of patients I've had.

B. I think you have to get rid of a lot of fancy expectations and get down to reality with these people. I try to keep in mind what goes into being an alcoholic. There was a guy in one of our groups—he was sort of living in a bar and actually panhandling the other members of the group for money for drinking. It seemed like he was getting even with the dominant culture. He can teach us something and we can teach him—it's a good kind of exchange.

D. A couple of things influenced me into working with alcoholics and I think helped me do it pretty well in addition to my training as a psychologist. I had two very close friends who were

From an unpublished taped interview.

alcoholics and they were both very bright, very sensitive, and I had known them for a number of years and seen the repetitive pattern—like swearing that they would never drink again and they always did. So I wasn't so surprised and shocked. And I had some work experience outside—in a bank, driving a cab, and so on.

A. I've thought back a lot to my last job. It was a lot more sort of businesslike than this. You need an artificial leg to be able to work, we'll buy you one and then you will get to work. It was easy—you send the guy to the doctor, the doctor gets him fitted with a leg, you've accomplished something. You can see it and so can he and he thanks you a lot and that's that. Only it wasn't. The guy didn't always go to work only I could forget about him because I'd done my job.

E. I think this is a lot more definite than what I used to do—marriage counseling. Those people had a lot of problems but they could never tell you what they were or what they wanted you to help them with. But here I enjoy it when people come here and say I have this problem—like drugs—and I want help with it. I find them pretty truthful and friendly—when they see me on the street at lunchtime or something they come over and say Hi. Clients with domestic problems don't do that.

C. One thing I know, it's like nursing—you can't save everybody. There was this man I saw for a time—he had a manslaughter charge against him, he was sent by the court. He kept saying "I'm doing much better" but he just was keeping on drinking and doing a lot of other things he knew he shouldn't. But at the same time I think throughout his whole life he has been pampered and babied and anything he'd done he's gotten away with and I think if we had said well maybe he can make it, and if we could have gotten him off it would have just been another thing he'd gotten away with and this was killing a person, you know. And should he be allowed to continue this way? What's he going to do next? I think some place along the line he's got to face up to what he is doing.

It was hard, 'cause I'd like to keep a guy out of prison. I'd hate to think of him—you know—if this is where it's going to lead. We just wrote the letter this morning—Well, of course, he feels that I wasn't helping him the way I should.

I think I'm helping him—I'm doing what I have to do, whether it helps him or hurts him. I think in the long run it will help him more than if I jumped on his bandwagon and did what he wanted.

F. I was with Public Welfare and there you're not so directly involved with change—you sort of accept that you'll get to some people and not to others. I think you have to do that here, too. I've pretty much accepted that not everyone who comes in contact with me down here is going to get better. Though sometimes I still get kind of angry and then you get punitive. I sort of want to say, well, you have to live up to the regulations or I won't have anything to do with you.

C. I think what's hardest for me—there are so few facilities to help you. Like even a lot of hospitals won't take alcoholics—just say throw them in the drunk tank if they're too drunk to treat here. And if they want training or even employment in something they know how to do—you know a lot of alcoholics are very good at their jobs when they aren't drinking—you can't get it for them. It makes you feel awfully helpless when no one will give them a chance.

F. Yeah—but they don't help themselves much sometimes. Like with taking a pill—antabuse or methadone—they cheat on you sometimes if they can. They've got a lot of ways—don't swallow the antabuse or methadone, just keep it under their tongue and like that. I'll admit its hard for me to go on working with a girl or a man who deliberately tries to deceive me.

B. But it's like the doctor says—you got to look at it like, a ball player doesn't expect to hit a home run every time. If he makes it once in fifty times, he can go on trying.

Little more needs to be added to suggest that human service workers in the newly developing field of service to addicts face many difficulties and must be able to derive from a small number of successes the courage and the will to continue to make a large personal investment in their work.

This chapter has attempted to present a sample of institutional settings and the people who work in them that are likely to be found today in all parts of this country. But it should be remembered that although they have the longest history of organized human services, which would suggest that they are least subject to change, the fact is that institutional services are changing rapidly and may look quite different in the next decade. Trends toward smaller units are strong, both because these units give promise of providing the best kind of contacts between helping people and people who need help and because the cost of operating large institutions is becoming prohibitive. Communities, though far from as welcoming as they might be, are becoming increasingly aware of the need to accept deviant individuals as part of their daily lives rather than to wall them off where natural contacts are impossible. This time of dynamic change will be an interesting one for human service workers though it will also involve the need to develop new skills and new ways of using familiar ones.

Although there is a hopeful and important shift in emphasis today from institutionalization in large, congregate facilities to smaller units, there remain many large institutions which employ human service workers at every level of competence. This chapter has discussed some of them but lack of space has allowed no mention of others, such as those for the severely mentally retarded. Recognition continues to grow that human relationships are the major means of helping the people in institutional settings, large and small, to find their way into a life in the community that is satisfying to themselves and acceptable to their society. This means that there will continue to be a large demand for human service workers in all kinds of group living settings, and that they will be expected to have direct helping relationships with those who live there far beyond providing them with the daily physical necessities of life. This field of work, never an easy one, may be less stressful for human service workers now than in the past because they will have more contacts with other professional members of the staff and because they will not be so physically isolated from the community. It will add to the tasks of the human service worker the responsibility for interpreting to the community at large what he knows of the people and their needs in the institution he serves.

questions

It has been suggested that even the most routine questions asked to obtain basic information for agency records may arouse different feelings in different individuals which, in turn, may influence their answers. What might be the reaction and response to requests for information about residence, parents' names, and occupation of Wayne, Deborah, and Joe?

It has been said that distress signals are sometimes sent by individuals who do not understand that they are sending them, and then decoded and answered by the experienced human service worker all without verbal communication. Describe some instances of this kind of communication from this chapter. Identify some instances where signals went unheeded or were misinterpreted.

Suggest some alternative ways in which some of the problems of the human service workers and individuals in their care described in this chapter might have been handled.

additional reading

Burmeister, Eva. *Tough Times and Tender Moments in Child Care Work.* 1967. New York: Columbia University Press, 1967. Human service workers interested in work with children in general will find it worthwhile to read this entire book from which the excerpt about Wayne is taken. It centers around the experiences of child care staff in residential settings but has wide applicability to all children who have had to be separated from their parents and the staff that has to deal with their unhappiness, anger and fear.

Green, Hannah. *I Never Promised You a Rose Garden.* New York: Holt, Rinehart and Winston, 1964. It would be worthwhile to a human service worker interested in work with the mentally ill to read the whole novel from which the excerpt about Deborah quoted in this chapter is taken. It gives an ongoing account of Deborah's illness, its effect on her family and their effect on her, her struggle to return to normal life, as well as many pictures of daily life in the hospital. It follows her through periods of acute mental illness, convalescence, and relapse and affords the human service worker insights into the hearts and minds of many other mentally ill individuals that are not found in many books.

Collins, Alice H. *The Lonely and Afraid: Counseling the Hard to Reach.* New York: Odyssey Press, 1969. As its name implies, this book is intended for the use of human service workers in contact with people like Joe who are constantly in difficulties with their society largely through their own acts, but who seem to reject the help they so obviously need. The book suggests some of the dynamics which may underlie their behavior and some techniques which can be useful in helping them. The second part of the book consists of readings in theory and some additional case examples drawn from the past as well as the present, pertinent to fuller understanding of the theory and practice described in the first part of the book.

summary

Hopefully, the foregoing pages have served as an introduction to the human services, to the kinds of skills needed to work well in them, and to some of the people to be met there as colleagues and as users. An introduction it should be remembered, is just a first step which may or may not lead to more exploration. An impression, gained at introduction, may be confirmed or contradicted on closer acquaintance.

There is obviously much more to be learned about the human services than what has been told in this book. Personality and learning theories on which practice may be based have hardly been mentioned. Only a few of the many kinds of human services have been briefly described here, and those that have made an appearance may look quite different in the near future, as new ways of giving services are organized and tested.

One of the most interesting, though sometimes baffling aspects of the human services is that they are dynamic—they change as social conditions change and new learning becomes available. For those who like change, this is indeed one of their most attractive aspects. The increasing emphasis on research in the human services may attract to that specialty individuals who are interested in the field but not prepared for the endless adjustments it demands. For others this introduction may serve best if it permits them to decide against further contact with the human service field.

Those who have found the study of this field worth pursuing further may do so in a number of ways. They may increase their theoretical knowledge with further study in the behavioral sciences —sociology, psychology, anthropology. Or they may learn more about the background of present-day life from a study of the humanities—history, literature, philosophy. Those who have discovered a specific field of interest, such as education or medicine, may want to undertake specialized work in it. Urban studies and public administration are subjects that prospective human service workers will find valuable. And since it is clear that in the future the use of electronic systems will play an increasingly important part in freeing people to work with people, prospective human service workers may find it useful to gain a basic understanding of computers and statistical methods.

However, the theoretical is sometimes of less interest than the practical to those attracted to the human services. This work makes a strong appeal to individuals who want to "do something" and who may want to do it without waiting to complete a long period of theoretical education. As must be clear from the foregoing pages, there is room for such persons in the human services just as there is a place for those with more formal training. Unfortunately, it is not practical to draw up a blueprint here of work possibilities and the necessary educational achievements for them, although this kind of diagram would be helpful to prospective human service workers. The constantly changing nature of the work makes it impossible to predict what jobs will exist six months from now in any one city, much less in fifty states.

A few general statements are ventured, in the light of present trends. Those with postgraduate training will most probably continue to receive the top salaries and will, in general, carry major administrative responsibility. They are likely to be found increasingly in supervisory, consultative, and educational positions with a corresponding reduction in the amount of their firsthand contact with service consumers. Graduates of four-year college programs are likely to have direct contact with these consumers, under supervision of those with postgraduate training. Two-year community college certification programs in many human service fields are growing rapidly. Their graduates are likely to find places as members of teams, in newly created jobs, as special interpreters for cultural groups they understand exceptionally well, or all three. Individuals with a high school education, or sometimes without, who have unusual talent will also be recruited onto human service teams. Volunteers (individuals who offer their services without salary) are likely to continue to be in demand because they bring a special kind of enthusiasm and point of view to the work and because the need for helping people is likely to continue to far outstrip the funds available for employing them.

There is no better way of testing out a first impression of the human services than by firsthand acquaintance. It has been suggested that an excellent investment for a student is employment in the human services during summer vacations or in part-time work in conjunction with study. Today, when students are not necessarily recent high school graduates, individuals seeking new careers or occupations can also make excellent use of a period of student employment in a human service agency. Agencies whose work load is heavy and labor turnover high, are most likely to accept such students as temporary employees. This arrangement is all to the good for the individual who wants to find out if he really has an aptitude or interest in this kind of work. He will find himself in a real and difficult work situation, not a protected or artificial one, and he will learn quickly what the drawbacks, frustrations, and problems of the work may be. If then, he is still interested and excited about becoming a human service worker he will have made his decision on the basis of intimate acquaintance.

Finding work in the human services is in itself sometimes a test of the interest and perseverance of the individual seeking it. In many instances the public employment and civil service offices can help him. In others, he may need to find a listing of local human service agencies, perhaps through a community council or information service, and, having decided on the situations that interest him, make personal contacts with them. The availability of jobs is often dependent on the state of the economy in general. Agencies not infrequently find themselves in the painful position of needing the help a prospective human service worker wants to give but without funds to employ him. Their response to his application, then, may be colored by their feelings of frustration and the pressure of work they are under. It is a good test of the true interest of the prospective human service worker if he can, in spite of disappointments, continue to look for a job in the human services or accept one that is not his first choice and do it well.

This introduction has tried to show some of the range of possibilities for work in the human services, the kinds of temperament and learning needed for success there, and the satisfactions and difficulties to be found. If the reader follows up the book with firsthand acquaintance with the field, he will have a firm base for deciding if it will offer him the satisfaction he needs and enable him to make a contribution toward the well-being of others. If he turns to other fields of work, perhaps he will have been helped in his role as a citizen seeking a greater awareness of social problems and their solutions.

DATE DUE

FEB 8	JAN 21 '86		
DE 12'85	DEC 9 '85		

DEMCO 38-297